Diversity and the Effective Corporate Board

Diversity and the Effective Corporate Board

Ram Kumar Mishra
Shital Jhunjhunwala

AMSTERDAM • BOSTON • HEIDELBERG • LONDON
NEW YORK • OXFORD • PARIS • SAN DIEGO
SAN FRANCISCO • SINGAPORE • SYDNEY • TOKYO
Academic Press is an imprint of Elsevier

Academic Press is an imprint of Elsevier
The Boulevard, Langford Lane, Kidlington, Oxford, OX5 1GB, UK
25 Wyman Street, Waltham, MA 02451, USA

First published 2013

Notices

Knowledge and best practice in this field are constantly changing. As new research and
experience broaden our understanding, changes in research methods, professional practices,
or medical treatment may become necessary.

Practitioners and researchers must always rely on their own experience and knowledge in
evaluating and using any information, methods, compounds, or experiments described herein.
In using such information or methods they should be mindful of their own safety and the safety
of others, including parties for whom they have a professional responsibility.

To the fullest extent of the law, neither the Publisher nor the authors, contributors, or editors,
assume any liability for any injury and/or damage to persons or property as a matter of products
liability, negligence or otherwise, or from any use or operation of any methods, products,
instructions, or ideas contained in the material herein.

British Library Cataloguing in Publication Data
A catalogue record for this book is available from the British Library

Library of Congress Cataloging-in-Publication Data
A catalog record for this book is available from the Library of Congress

ISBN: 978-0-12-410497-6

For information on all Academic Press publications
visit our website at **store.elsevier.com**

This book has been manufactured using Print On Demand technology. Each copy is produced
to order and is limited to black ink. The online version of this book will show color figures
where appropriate.

Working together
to grow libraries in
developing countries

www.elsevier.com • www.bookaid.org

DEDICATION

To my loving parents, caring husband, and my darling daughter

Shital Jhunjhunwala

To Adi, Yashaswini and Divi

Ram Kumar Mishra

CONTENTS

INTRODUCTION

The performance of corporate boards has been a matter of great concern. Boards need to create long-term shareholder value while protecting the interest of all other stakeholders. They need to provide a return on investment on a regular basis yet ensure the long-term sustainability of the organization. Being a top performer in a highly complex and competitive environment is a major challenge. One significant factor influencing board performance is its composition, that is, the types of directors who form the board. There is a growing consensus that diversity in board composition is necessary for effective board performance.

This book discusses the various aspects of diversity affecting corporate boards, in terms of gender, age, nationality, tenure, education, experience, and personalities. It describes the need for diversity in each category, as well as concerns that may arise from such diversity. The book is supported by a large bank of statistics around diversity across the world. In addition, a detailed analysis of different aspects of board diversity in Singapore and India is presented.

CHAPTER 1

Diversity—Toward an Effective Board

"Diversity is the art of thinking independently together"
—Malcolm Stevenson Forbes, Publisher of *Forbes* magazine

1.1 CORPORATE BOARDS

A board of directors is a group of persons elected or appointed by the shareholders to oversee the activities of a company. They are entrusted with the overall direction of the enterprise. The board's powers and duties are determined by corporate laws and the bylaws of the organization.

Does the board actually run the business? The company is owned by shareholders, who elect the board of directors to act as trustees and

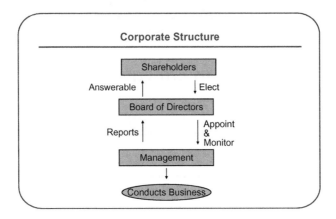

Fig. 1.1. Corporate Structure.

protect their investment and interests. The board of directors in turn appoints the management team, who have operational responsibility of the organization. The management periodically reports to the board of directors on the functioning of the organization. The board is answerable to the shareholders (see Figure 1.1).

The responsibility of the board is to "manage the organization," and the responsibility of managers (i.e. the CEO and his team) is to "manage the day-to-day activities or work of the organization" based on guidelines, policies, and objectives laid down by the board.

The objective of a company is long-term growth and sustainability. To this end, as representatives of the shareholders, the purpose of the board it is to oversee the functioning of the organization and ensure that it continues to operate in the best interests of all stakeholders. The roles of a corporate board of directors are three-fold (Figure 1.2) to:

- Govern
- Direct
- Supervise

1. The board is responsible for governance, that is, ensuring the organization operates properly and effectively, and achieves its agreed objectives. Governance involves:
   - Setting a framework, system, procedures, and policies that fulfills the objectives of the organization and needs of all stakeholders

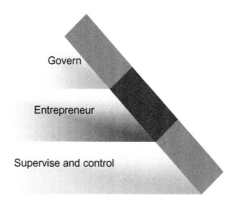

Fig. 1.2. Role of Board.

- Building the ethos and values that underpin the organization, enabling and ensuring transparent and accountable decision making
- Compliance with the laws and regulatory environment
2. The directors are responsible for giving strategic direction to the organization. This entrepreneurial role involves:
   - Maintaining a long-term overview of the organization and all its work
   - Making strategic and major decisions toward achieving the organization's objectives
   - Establishing operational policies and providing adequate resources for business activities
   - Appointing the CEO and management team and establishing management goals
3. Finally, the directors must constantly monitor the progress of the company toward its objectives as defined by shareholders. Supervising encompasses:
   - Establishing control and accountability systems that enable risk to be assessed and managed
   - Monitoring use of the firm's resources or wealth
   - Assessing the progress of implementation of the strategy
   - Monitoring management activities and achievement of the targets that are set

These roles require directors to hold three perspectives (Figure 1.3).

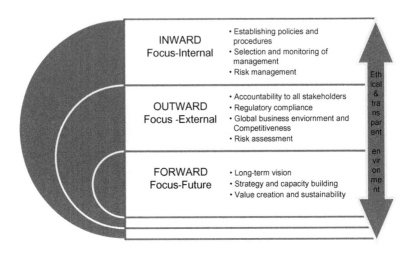

Fig. 1.3. Directors' Perspectives and Role.

The inward perspective allows directors to create the necessary policies and processes within the organization and choose the right people to run the business smoothly.

The outward dimension requires directors to step outside the organization and take care of the concerns of government, customers, and society at large. By looking at what's happening around them, the board will be able to appreciate the external environment and its impact on company's business.

A forward-looking board will be able to build the long-term vision and strategy for the company. Although no one may be able to see the future, it is the role of the board to make certain that the necessary capabilities in terms of people, intellectual property, and processes are in place for the company to face new challenges.

This requires a perceptive, level-headed, and well-balanced board with clairvoyant-like abilities. Only a very vibrant and multiperspective board can successfully carry out such a wide range of responsibilities.

1.2 BOARD DIVERSITY—A MUST FOR EFFECTIVE BOARD PERFORMANCE

The performance of corporate boards is dependent on directors effectively executing their roles and carrying out their responsibilities.

Board dynamism has been a matter of great concern of late. A company's success and long-term survival is dependent on the board's decisions. These decisions impact shareholders, employees, customers, and all other stakeholders. Being a top performer in a highly complex and competitive environment is a major challenge.

To achieve this, the board must comprehend the global environment, political and economic conditions in different countries, the industry's competitiveness and nuances, the market situation, financial and legal aspects, and the latest technology, and it must have the ability to innovate and overcome challenges faced in turbulent times. Thus, the board must possess a wide range of knowledge, expertise, skills, and perspectives. Such "completeness" is possible if the directors come from different backgrounds in terms of education, experience, nationality, and time periods.

Thus, a significant factor influencing board performance is its composition—the type of directors who form the board. There is a growing consensus that diversity in board composition is necessary for effective board performance.

Board diversity refers to the heterogeneous composition of the board in terms of gender, age, race, education, experience, nationality, lifestyle, culture, religion, and many other facets that make each of us unique as individuals.

A well-performing board needs diversity of knowledge, skills, and perspectives. Dr. Yılmaz Argüden [1] rightly commented that if everybody thinks in the same way, what is the need of a board? It may as well be a one-man show. Diversity for its own sake, however, is not an improvement in governance; what matters is the combination of complementary talents and experiences of the members that enables boards to steer the company toward success and long-term stability.

1.3 RATIONALE FOR BOARD DIVERSITY

"The test of a first-rate [board] intelligence is the ability to hold two opposing ideas in mind at the same time, and still retain the ability to function."
F. Scott Fitzgerald [2]

Great ideas come from differences. Differences can be created by diversity among the directors—demographic (gender, race), multi-disciplinary, and functional, and in terms of roles (visionary, executor). Scholars and regulators have been advocating board diversity as leading to enhanced board effectiveness, thereby improving corporate success. Heterogeneous boards with dissimilar opinions and approaches foster critical thinking and creative problem solving to effect better decision making, allow active monitoring, and boost strategic direction—all the components essential for corporate success.

1.3.1 Rationale 1: Innovation and Creative Problem Solving
People from different backgrounds and with different life experiences are likely to approach similar problems in different ways. Evidence indicates that more diverse groups foster creativity and produce a greater range of perspectives and solutions to problems. That is, diverse groups are less likely to suffer from *groupthink.*

1.3.2 Rationale 2: Acquiring Talent and Employee Relationships
Companies are facing a talent crunch that goes right up to the top. Hiring women, minorities, and people from different parts of the world can increase the talent pool of corporate boards. A diverse board facilitates policies and procedures that increase hiring and improve the management of diverse employees.

1.3.3 Rationale 3: Understanding the Business Marketplace
Exposure of the organization to a wide variety of cultures, ideas, and views at every level, including the board, is needed to meet the demands of increasingly diverse employees, customers, and clients. A heterogeneous board will have a better understanding of the marketplace, increasing sales performance and hence profitability. Together with a diverse employee base they will be able to customize products and services to the specific needs of diverse communities and penetrate new markets. "Homogeneity at the top of a company is believed to result in a narrow perspective while diverse top managers take a broader view. The result of diversity at the top is a better understanding of the complexities of the environment and more astute decisions" [3].

1.3.4 Rationale 4: Access to Resources and Networks
A primary responsibility of the board is building external linkages and acquiring resources for the firm. By selecting directors with different characteristics, firms may gain access to different resources. For instance, directors with financial industry experience can help firms

gain access to specific investors. Directors with political connections may help firms deal with regulators or win government procurement contracts. Dissimilar group members may also contribute by acquiring information through a more diverse set of sources. For example, minority members' networks may give them access to unique sources of information.

1.3.5 Rationale 5: Reputation Enhancer

Including women, minorities (ethnic, religious, etc.), and stakeholders' representatives (employees, suppliers, or minority shareholders) on the board helps firms enhance their reputation as responsible citizens. They are perceived as companies that protect the interest of all stakeholders, gaining respect in the eyes of media, government, and the public at large.

Diversity, it is argued, enhances the effectiveness of corporate leadership. While the rationales described above provide business justification for board diversity, there is also a social argument. Appointment of women, minorities, and people of different social levels (i.e. from lower castes in the Indian context) on boards will be an affirmative action for social and economic advancement.

1.4 CONSTRAINTS OF BOARD DIVERSITY

Creating a diverse board can be a challenge in terms of finding competent people. Diverse boards, like any heterogeneous team, face the problem of establishing mutual trust and understanding among members.

1.4.1 Constraint 1: Group Conflict

The literature provides sufficient evidence that diversity increases conflict between subgroups. A key problem that arises is poor communication between team members. Communicating effectively with teammates who do not share a common technical language or perspective is a challenge [4]. Often the question of status or superiority creates conflict. Effective management of diversity on boards is necessary to achieve expected performance. Effort is required to increase group cohesiveness and improve the flow of communication. Higher expenditure is required for these initiatives. Demographic and functional diversity increase group conflict, reduce communication, and interfere with board functioning.

1.4.2 Constraint 2: Limited Talent

It may be found that few women, persons of lower social class (including caste in the Indian context), or minorities have the qualifications and experience needed for board-level appointment. Empirical research suggests that people who meet these requirements tend to hold multiple directorships. Thus, no one company gains a competitive edge by hiring them. Increased workload may also reduce their efficiency. As a result, finding suitable candidates may be difficult.

It is important not to appoint directors just for the sake of diversity. There is no point appointing a woman who does not have the necessary skill or experience to participate in board deliberations. It is essential to have a balanced board with the right candidates who can positively contribute to the board.

1.5 TYPES OF DIVERSITY

There are two broad categories of diversity: surface level and deep-level diversity. The surface level consists of observable and non-observable diversity. Deep-level diversity is concerned with personality diversity, including cognitive features—perceptions, values, and personal characteristics.

1.5.1 Observable Diversity

Attributes of directors that are easily determinable or visible fall under this category. *Demographic* factors such as race/ethnic background, nationality, gender, and age are examples of observable features.

1.5.1.1 Gender Diversity

Gender diversity refers to the proportion of females to males. Men and women behave differently. Women are believed to be more intuitive in decision making, have the ability to multitask, and are better at building relationships. Men tend to be more task focused and make decisions based on information and procedures.

1.5.1.2 Age Diversity

Age diversity indicates the mix of members of different ages. Younger people are perceived to be more flexible, have a better appreciation of new concepts and technologies, and are higher risk takers. They have the ability to grasp complex mathematical models and a deep understanding of the ability, reach, and limitations of the Internet and online-based services. The board may, on the other hand, benefit from the wide experience of the senior members. Senior members often have strong networks and clout from which the company can leverage.

1.5.1.3 Regional Diversity
Regional diversity implies that the board has members from different nationalities. Companies are now part of a global economy, having business activities in different parts of the world. Having a board that understands how different countries operate, their business environments, and their people is a necessity. Further, people from different countries have different lifestyles, cultures, and family backgrounds that help bring new perspectives and solutions to the table.

1.5.1.4 Tenure Diversity
Diversity of tenure involves a balance between new and old directors. Having well-reputed directors on boards for a length of time improves corporate reputations. Directors who have been on the board for long periods, likely will have a good understanding of the company, but this may run the risk of directors not keeping up with changes needed in the business and defending decisions that may not be appropriate in the present situation. It can also affect the independence of directors. A fresh pair of eyes always brings with it a new perspective.

1.5.1.5 Race/Ethnic/Community/Class/Religion Diversity
The literature mostly discusses racial and ethnic diversity in boards given the social structure of countries like the United States, Singapore, and Malaysia. It suggests that people of all racial and ethnic groups should be represented on the board. In the Indian context, the idea may be extended to include any social stratification such as religion or caste.

*Race** refers to a person's physical appearance, such as skin color, eye color, hair color, and so on. *Ethnicity* refers to groups sharing a common language, cultural heritage, traditions, beliefs, and rituals. *Religion* involves a set of beliefs that are spiritual in nature and is specially considered with creation of a superhuman agency. In India, the

---

*This explanation of terms given is very broad and purely operational for purposes of this study of board diversity. These are not definitions or accurate meanings.

concept of *community* refers to language and state of origin, another way in which groups in society exist—Bengalis, Gujaratis, Tamils, and so on. They share a common language and culture and are similar to ethnic groups. The *caste* system is also prevalent in India, originally as a classification according to one's function and occupation in society, but now considered hereditary.

Boards typically have directors from the same social background (community, religion, etc.) as the promoters in nongovernmental organizations. Including socially diverse directors on board will help broaden the perspectives and experience of the whole team. Majority members may stigmatize the minorities, making it difficult for them to perform to their potential. An open and supportive environment should be created. It is important that the minorities be selected not just as tokens but rather on the basis of being competent people who are treated as peers so that they can effectively contribute to board activities.

1.5.2 Nonobservable Diversity
Nonobservable diversity relates to attributes that are less visible, such as educational qualifications, expertise, and experience.

1.5.2.1 Multidisciplinary
Multidisciplinary boards are expected to be useful in decisions that are high in complexity and have many interdependent subtasks. Members with complementary education, knowledge, and skills can take a more comprehensive approach to problem solving. Research indicates that teams that are multidisciplinary tend to be more innovative.

1.5.2.2 Cross-Functional
Members with a varied of experience—for example, in terms of functional, industry-specific, or specialized skills—look at problems differently and focus on different aspects of issues under consideration. This leads to creative problem solving and innovative decision making.

1.5.3 Personality Diversity
The personality of an individual is framed by his or her attitudes, attributes, social endowment, and skills. Each person has his or her way of thinking and doing things. Some are introverts, others are extroverts. Some like to look at the big picture; others are more comfortable with details and numbers. People with various personal traits will help

board members carry out different responsibilities on the team and play a variety of roles in the decision-making process.

We shall discuss these diversity features in more details in the following chapters, with special reference to India and Singapore.

REFERENCES

[1] Y. Argüden, Diversity at The Head Table, Bringing Complementary Skills and Experiences to the Board, Private Sector Opinion 19, A Global Corporate Governance Forum Publication.

[2] M. Hilb, New corporate governance: from good guidelines to great practice, Corp Gov 13(5) (2005) 580.

[3] D.A. Carter, B.J. Simkins, W. Gary Simpson, Corporate governance, board diversity and firm value, Financ Rev 38(33−53) (2003) 36.

[4] S.E. Jackson, The consequences of diversity in multidisciplinary work teams, Handbook of Work Group Psychology, John Wiley & Sons Ltd., 1996, pp. 53−75.

CHAPTER 2

Women on Boards

Although women have become significant contributors to the economy, there are very few women leading companies as board members. This chapter examines the reasons for the small number of women on boards and elucidates why it is important to have women as an integral part of boards.

2.1 MEN STILL DOMINATE BOARDS

Women in the United States make up 47.3% [1] of the labor force and 51.4% [2] of management, professional, and related positions, yet only 15.7% [2] of board members are women. Australian women comprise 50.2% of the population, nearly 50% of the workforce, 56% of all higher education students, and 55% of all university graduates, yet form only 12.5% of directors of Australia's top 200 companies [3]. Globally 9.8% [4] of directors are women, with only 58.3% [4] of all companies having a female on board. Women have climbed Mt. Everest and travelled to the moon, but when it comes to boardrooms, they are few and far between. Discrimination against women as corporate leaders, even in the most progressive of countries, is evidenced by the graph (Figure 2.1). Boards still recently were considered a "boys' club," with more than 40% of companies still having an all-male board. Across continents, the representation of women on boards is far from acceptable. Although in four European countries (Norway, Sweden, Finland, and France) women occupy more than 20% of the seats, in other countries including the United States, UK, Germany, and New Zealand, women representation on boards is only between 8% and 16%. These countries are in the list of top 25 countries (Figure 2.1). The proportion of women in developed economies like Japan (0.9%), UAE (1.2%), and the BRIC nations—Brazil (5.1%), Russia (5.9%), and India (4.8%)—is minimal. Several countries such as Peru and Morocco have only all-male boards (Figure 2.2).

2.2 WHY SO FEW WOMEN?

2.2.1 Demand Barriers

The bias or prejudice against women that they cannot perform as well as men in top-level corporate jobs is probably the single most important reason for boards still remaining male dominated. Described as the *glass ceiling effect*, it constitutes an invisible barrier that women face in the path to the top. It is "the unseen, yet unbreachable barrier that keeps... women from rising to the upper rungs of the corporate ladder, regardless of their qualifications or achievements" [5]. It indicates a gender inequality that is greater at higher levels compared to lower levels, blocking the advancement of women to positions of power or prestige, particularly in the corporate world. Although gender discrimination is unlawful in India, the United States, and most developed countries, it still occurs in different dimensions of society. Women are simply not considered for a position on the board. Exclusion from the "boys' club" is one of the biggest issues faced by women. "Those individuals (men) who occupy the top positions have a stake in maintaining traditional rules and procedures related to hiring, promotion, seniority, and other personnel practices, that work to their advantage and exclude others" [6]. This is a manifestation of "conscious and unconscious stereotyping, prejudice, and bias related to gender" [7]. According to Ann Morrison [8], of all the barriers to corporate advancement identified, it is prejudice that tops the list, the

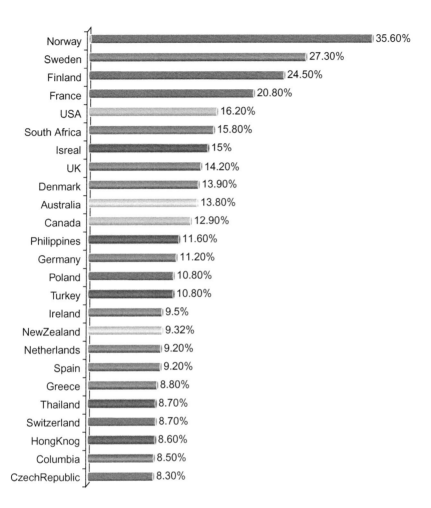

Norway	35.60%
Sweden	27.30%
Finland	24.50%
France	20.80%
USA	16.20%
South Africa	15.80%
Isreal	15%
UK	14.20%
Denmark	13.90%
Australia	13.80%
Canada	12.90%
Philippines	11.60%
Germany	11.20%
Poland	10.80%
Turkey	10.80%
Ireland	9.5%
NewZealand	9.32%
Netherlands	9.20%
Spain	9.20%
Greece	8.80%
Thailand	8.70%
Switzerland	8.70%
HongKnog	8.60%
Columbia	8.50%
CzechRepublic	8.30%

▪ Europe ▪ Asia ▪ Nort America ▪ South America   Australia ▪ Africa

Fig. 2.1. Women on Boards – Top 25 countries. Source: Developed by the authors.

prejudgment that someone "different," such as a female executive, is less able to do the job.

Women are by and large offered lower-paying jobs. Women with equivalent or even higher qualifications, talent, and experience than their male competitors are generally not even regarded as a possible choice for senior management positions. In addition, companies perceive women executives to be less committed to the company and their own career growth. Developing women for high-level positions is

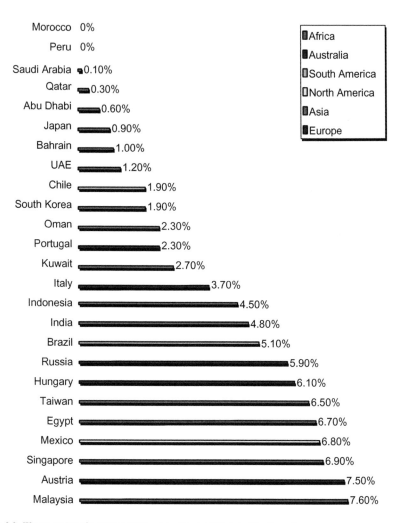

Fig. 2.2. Women on Boards: Bottom 25 Countries. Source: Developed by the authors.

considered a risky investment that may be lost if they leave to meet family responsibilities.

2.2.2 Supply Barriers

The biggest supply barrier to female directors is a paucity of qualified women with the necessary professional knowledge and skills. Inflexible and long work schedules and excessive travel often restrict women in the pursuit of career advancement. The small number of women with experience at a senior level shrinks the population from which to select female board members. As women have only recently made an

Fig. 2.3. Board with Complementary Skills. Source: Developed by the authors.

appearance in senior management positions, there are hardly any women with the necessary experience to join boards.

Women often do not have mentors to guide them or role models to emulate. Men avoid mentoring women out of fear that their relationship will be considered personal, and there are simply not enough women at the top to mentor female board aspirants.

2.3 WHY WE NEED WOMEN ON BOARDS

Men and women behave differently. Women are believed to be capable of multitasking, be more intuitive in decision making, and better at building relationships. Men, on the other hand, are assumed to be more task focused and analytical in the decision-making process. Women, it is argued, are less likely to avoid controversial issues and ask the tough questions to improve the quality of decision making. Women, by being good listeners and facilitating a win–win approach, are able to reduce board conflict and improve board room dynamics (see Figure 2.3).

Men, with their short-term and more performance-oriented approach, ensure that the company's goals are achieved. Male directors with an autocratic leadership style are able to exercise better control on management. The democratic leadership style of women encourages multiple views from different stakeholders. By their cooperative approach and long-term perspective, women directors are able to build positive and lasting relationships with management, customers, shareholders, and other stakeholders, thereby helping boards manage risk and be socially more responsible.

Gender diversity (equal proportion of females to males) has a positive effect on boards. The McKinsey report, *Women Matter 2* [9], found that women are more likely to apply leadership behaviors involving people development, expectations and rewards, and role modeling that have a positive effect on organizational performance. Men, on the other hand, adopt individualistic decision making and control, and corrective action leadership behaviors.

Women are increasingly becoming a major driver of the economy, both as contributors and as customers; it is appropriate that they be a part of the team leading companies. In the United States, women are the economic powerhouse, influencing 95% [10] of all products and services sold. Women currently drive 70% of purchasing decisions in Europe, even though they account for only 51% of population [11]. Women now form 51% of the UK population and 46% of the economically active workforce [12]. They are estimated to be responsible for about 70% [12] of household purchasing decisions. Women are becoming influential even in traditionally male-dominated areas such as the buying of cars. Thus, women are likely to better understand consumer behavior, the needs of different segments, and identifying opportunities for companies in satisfying these needs. Having women as board members can result in new products, a larger customer base, and higher customer satisfaction, translating into greater market share and more earnings.

Female directors are believed to be better at monitoring. By not being one of the "old boys," they are likely to be more independent. Women board members are known to have better attendance records, forcing improved attendance by men.

Boards with more women members act as a motivator to other women employees within the organization. Female directors are able to create a more women-friendly work environment in the company, reducing gender discrimination and the incidence of sexual harassment.

Evidence shows that increased participation of women on boards enhances corporate performance. In 2004 [13] and 2007 [14], the U.S.-based business, Catalyst, reported that boards with the most female representatives outperformed those with the least women representation in terms of return on equity, return on sales, and return on capital employed. The Reibey Institute of Australia in June 2011 [15] found that over three- and five-year periods, ASX500 companies with women directors delivered significantly higher return on equity (ROE) than those companies without any women on their boards.

Reputation and investor confidence may improve with the addition of women to a company's board. Institutional investors such as CalPERS (USA) and Amazone (Europe) are giving weight to gender diversity in their investment selections. Rating agencies such as Innovest and Vigeo are also adding gender diversity as a criterion to evaluate organizational excellence and corporate governance.

Companies are facing a huge talent crunch that goes right up to the board level. Broadening the talent pool by including women directors will help boards get skilled and competent members with a diversity of perspectives and leadership styles, who can significantly contribute to board performance.

2.4 GENDER DIVERSITY—ON THE MOVE

The ratio of women directors has been increasing slowly but steadily over the years. Globally, the percentage of women on boards has increased from 9.2% [16] in 2009 to 9.6% [4] in 2011, with 58% [4] of boards now having at least one female director. The increase in participation of women on boards has been more pronounced in Europe, from 5% in 2001 [17] to 8% in 2004 [18] to 9.7% in 2008 [19] to 12% [20] in 2011. There has been a steady increase in gender diversity, with participation of women on board almost doubling in the last two decades. In countries such as the UK, United States, Canada, Norway, Finland, Sweden, and Switzerland, 80–90% of boards have at least one female member. Asian countries such as India and Singapore have yet to cross the 50% mark (see Table 2.1).

Table 2.1. Women on Board: The Global Picture

		1993	1995	1996	1997	1998	1999	2000	2001	2002	2003	2004	2005	2006	2007	2008	2009	2010	2011
USA	Women	8.30%	9.5%	10.2%	10.6%	11.1%	11.2%	11.7%	12.4%	12.8%	13.6%	14.3%	14.7%	14.6%	14.8%	15.2%	15.2%	15.7%	16.1%
	Boards	69.0%	80.8%	83.0%	84.0%	86.0%	84.0%	86.0%	87.0%	82.0%	89.2%	88.0%	89.4%	88.4%	88.2%	86.8%	87.7%	87.9%	88.7%
	Sample		Fort 500	Fort 500	Fort 500	Fort 500	Fort 500	Fort 500	Fort 500	S&P 500	Fort 500	S&P 500	Fort 500	Fort 500	Fort 500	Fort 500	Fort 500	Fort 500	Fort 500
Italy	Women	2.5%	3.1%	3.2%	3.3%	3.4%	3.8%	4.1%	4.2%	4.3%	4.3%	4.5%	4.6%	4.7%	5.4%	2.1%	3.8%	3.9%	3.7%
	Boards													22.0%	60.5%	30.0%	41.2%	35.7%	34.6%
	Sample	>200	>200	>200	>200	>200	>200	>200	>200	>200	>200	>200		EWM	296	EWM 23	GMI 51	GWM 23	GMI 52
Netherlands	Women			2.5%				3.1%	4.0%	4.0%	3.4%	3.4%	3.6%	5.1%		7.0%	7.7%	8.1%	9.2%
	Boards																41.2%	41.2%	45.6%
	Sample			NBI 100				NBI 100	NBI 100	NBI 100		NBI 100	NBI 100	NBI 100	NBI 100	NBI 100	Euronext 9	Euronext 9	E7uronext 9
New Zealand	Women				4.4%	4.9%	4.9%	5.9%	5.7%			5.0%		7.1%		8.7%	12.0%	9.3%	7.5%
	Boards				28.30%							28.0%		37.0%		40.0%	66.7%	43.0%	35.0%
	Sample				166	59	59	59	59			NZSX 100	NZSX 100	NZSX 100		NZSX 100	GMI 12	NZSX 100	Korn 100
Canada	Women					9.0%	9.0%	10.0%	11.1%	11.4%	12.0%	12.6%	12.4%	13.0%	14.0%	15.0%	16.0%	16.0%	17.0%
	Boards					36.4%		71.0%	48.6%		79.0%	80.0%	85.0%	87.0%	83.0%	83.0%	81.0%	82.0%	88.0%
	Sample					FP	CBI 100	CBI 100	FP	CBI 100	CBI 100	CBI 100	CBI 100	CBI 100	CBI 100	CBI 100	CBI 100	CBI 100	CBI 100
UK	Women						6.3%	5.8%	6.4%	7.2%	8.6%	9.7%	10.5%	10.3%	11.0%	11.7%	12.2%	12.5%	14.2%
	Boards						64.0%	58.0%	57.0%	61.0%	68.0%	69.0%	78.0%	77.0%	76.0%	78.0%	75.0%	79.0%	
	Sample						FT 100	FT 100	FT 100	FT 100	FT 100	FT 100	FT 100	FT 100	FT 100	FT 100	FT 100	FT 100	FT 100
Hong Kong	Women						< 5%										8.9%	8.3%	8.6%
	Boards																66.7%	57.0%	57.0%
	Sample						HSI										HSI	GMI 79	Korn 100

Country												
Denmark	Women	7.9%	8.0%	7.5%	7.4%	7.1%	6.9%	7.8%	18.1%	13.1%	14.4%	13.9%
	Boards	37.5%	40.0%	34.5%	33.3%	35.0%	31.1%	35.3%	100.0%	76.9%	80.8%	79.2%
	Sample	104	110	119	120	120	135	133	EWM 6	GMI 26	GMI 26	GMI 24
Finland	Women	4.6%	4.5%	5.5%	7.2%	8.0%	10.1%	11.6%	25.7%	21.8%	23.4%	24.5%
	Boards	25.0%	25.0%	28.2%	33.7%	31.9%	42.6%	49.5%	100.0%	88.9%	96.3%	100.0%
	Sample	72	80	85	92	94	122	125	EWM 8	GMI 27	GMI 27	GMI 28
Norway	Women	8.5%	10.9%	13.1%	15.5%	21.1%	29.5%	39.1%	44.2%	35.8%	34.3%	35.6%
	Boards	34.4%	44.4%	49.4%	51.0%	73.1%	90.2%	96.5%	100.0%	91.3%	91.3%	96.0%
	Sample	64	72	79	89	104	132	144	EWM 6	GMI 23	GMI 23	GMI 25
Sweden	Women	6.7%	7.1%	10.5%	15.4%	15.8%	15.9%	18.4%	22.0%	24.0%	23.9%	27.3%
	Boards	37.7%	38.7%	49.5%	68.7%	72.2%	66.0%	76.8%	94.0%	94.0%	95.9%	100.0%
	Sample	191	209	210	217	217	368	276	SB 170	GMI 50	GMI 49	GMI 40
Australia	Women				8.6%		8.7%		8.3%	8.3%	10.7%	13.4%
	Boards GMI									56.8%	43.5%	55.3%
	Sample				ASX 200		ASX 200		ASX 200	ASX 200	ASX 200	ASX 200
South Africa	Women				7.1%	10.7%	11.5%	13.1%	14.3%	14.6%	16.6%	15.8%
	Boards									66.6%	78.5%	79.3%
	Sample				JSE 364	JSE 372	JSE 343	JSE 318	JSE 335	JSE 380	JSE 335	JSE 339
Spain	Women				3.5%	4.0%	6.2%	3.1%	7.6%	6.0%	8.00%	9.0%
	Boards					32.0%	40.2%		55.4%	57.0%	71.70%	74.0%
	Sample				EWM	119	SIBEX 130	IBEX 35	SIBEX 130	IBEX 35	GMI 46	IBEX 35
Germany	Women				10.0%		7.2%	12.4%	7.8%	10.4%	8.5%	11.2%
	Boards						72.0%		82.0%	64.2%	84.1%	70.4%
	Sample				EWM		EWM	DAX 30	EWM 44	GMI 95	EWM 44	GMI 81

(Continued)

Table 2.1. (Continued)

Country		1993	1995	1996	1997	1998	1999	2000	2001	2002	2003	2004	2005	2006	2007	2008	2009	2010	2011
France	Women											6.0%		7.6%	7.5%	7.6%	8.0%	12.0%	11.0%
	Boards												77.5%	75.0%		73.0%	77.0%	69.9%	90.0%
	Sample											EWM	40	EWM	CAC 40	EWM 56	CAC 40	EWM 56	CAC 40
Belgium	Women											3%		5.8%	5.3%	7%	8%	11.11	8%
	Boards													43%		44%	55%	66.7	65%
	Sample											EWM		EWM	BEL 19	EWM 9	BEL 20	EWM 9	BEL 20
Japan	Women												0.02				0.9%	0.9%	0.9%
	Boards												3%				8.8%	9.4%	9.9%
	Sample												2396				GMI 456	GMI 404	GMI 395
Portugal	Women													0.0%	0.7%	0.8%	3.0%	3.5%	4.0%
	Boards													0.0%		17.0%	30.0%	66.7%	45.0%
	Sample													EWM	H&S 10	EWM 6	PSI 20	EWM 6	PSI 20
Switzerland	Women													5.9%	7.2%	6.6%	9.0%	8.8%	11.0%
	Boards													58.0%		57.0%	65.0%	75.0%	85.0%
	Sample													EWM	H&S 20	EWM 23	SMI 50	EWM 24	SMI 50
Austria	Women													9.5%		9.2%	6.0%	12.5%	8.0%
	Boards													50.0%		50.0%	35.0%	83.0%	50.0%
	Sample													EWM		EWM 6	ATX 20	EWM 6	ATX 20
Singapore	Women															6.6%	5.8%	6.9%	6.4%
	Boards															38.0%	33.4%	38.7%	41.0%
	Sample															SGX listed	SGX listed	SGX listed	Korn 100

India	Women	4.2%	4.8%	4.7%
	Boards	38.9%	43.4%	43.0%
	Sample	GMI 54	GMI 53	Korn 100
China	Women	6.7%	7.2%	8.1%
	Boards	48.5%	48.7%	51.0%
	Sample	GMI 66	GMI 78	Korn 100
Israel	Women	12.9%	15.0%	13.4%
	Boards	88.2%	88.0%	100.0%
	Sample	GMI 17	Tel Aviv 10	GMI 17
Poland	Women	9.9%	7.4%	8.0%
	Boards	66.7%	50.0%	53.0%
	Sample	GMI 15	GMI 12	WSE 20
Russia	Women	6.3%	5.1%	5.9%
	Boards	44.0%	33.3%	38.5%
	Sample	GMI 25	GMI 24	GMI 26
Brazil	Women	4.4%	4.6%	5.1%
	Boards	30.5%	31.5%	33.8%
	Sample	GMI 59	GMI 54	GMI 74

Note: Table presents the proportion of women directors (Women) and percentage of companies whose boards have at least one woman (Boards) over the years based on different studies (Sample) across countries. Refer to notes at the end.

Sources: Refs. [4], [12], [16–19], [21–29], [30], [31–32], [33–41], [42–50].

Table 2.2. Change in Women's Proportion on Boards

Country	2001	2011	% Change
Finland	4.63%	24.50%	429%
Norway	8.45%	35.60%	321%
Sweden	6.71%	27.30%	307%
Netherlands	4.00%	9.20%	130%
UK	6.40%	14.20%	122%
Denmark	7.93%	13.90%	75%
Canada	11.10%	17.00%	53%
New Zealand	5.69%	7.50%	32%
USA	12.40%	16.10%	30%
Italy	4.20%	3.70%	−12%

Scandinavian countries have become the best performers in terms of female representation on boards, with an increase of more than 300% over the last decade. The United States and Canada have also shown an increase of 30% and 53% over the last ten years. Italy is probably the only country with a reverse trend, where the proportion of women on boards has actually fallen (see Table 2.2).

2.4.1 More the Merrier

It is not enough to appoint the "fairer sex" on boards. They should not just be symbolic representatves of their gender. Qualified and competent women should be appointed who can actively contribute to board effectiveness. It is important to build an open and supportive environment where women members can comfortably participate and their views are not marginalized. While even a single female director can make significant contributions, it is important that she be heard and not ignored or sidelined by the majority male members. Two female directors on a board would strengthen their position, and together they may have a better chance of being heard. Three or more women representatives on boards, popularly known as the "critical mass," will have a very strong impact on board functioning, as they will no longer represent the "women's view" but will become a "regular" board member (Figure 2.4), with a specific set of perspectives and skills.

In the global study of Fortune 200 [51] companies in 2009, 23% of boards had no women, 26% had only one woman director, 29% had

Fig. 2.4. Tokenism to Regular Member.
Note: Concept. Shital Jhunjhunwala; Design: A. Rakesh Phanindra.

two women directors, and 23% of boards had three or more female directors (Table 2.3). In Canada 12% of boards have four or more women directors, triple the number since 2000. However, in most countries, boards do not have four women members. The United

Table 2.3. Proportion of Companies with Women on Board

Country	Year	Study	4 or more women	3 women	2 women	1 woman	0 women
Canada	2011	CBI 100	12%	11%	28%	37%	12%
USA	2011	Fortune 1000	4%	11%	33%	36%	16%
Hong Kong	2011	Korn 100	2%	4%	20%	31%	43%
China	2011	Korn 100	1%	7%	14%	39%	39%
Malaysia	2011	Korn 100	1%	4%	13%	26%	56%
India	2011	Sensex 30	0%	3%	3%	44%	50%
Australia	2011	Korn 100	0%	1%	26%	44%	29%
New Zealand	2011	Korn 100	0%	1%	11%	23%	65%
Singapore	2011	STI 30	0%	0%	10%	38%	52%
Canada	2010	CBI 100	8%	12%	30%	32%	18%
Singapore	2010	All SGX	0%	1%	7%	31%	61%
USA	2009	S & P 500	5%	12%	36%	36%	11%
Hong Kong	2009	HSI 42	0%	2%	6%	92%	0%
Singapore	2009	All SGX	0%	1%	4%	28%	67%
Sweden	2008	SBI 70	6%	14%	37%	37%	6%
Singapore	2008	All SGX	0%	1%	6%	31%	62%
South Africa	2011	JSE 339		42%	19%	19%	21%
South Africa	2010	JSE 335		36%	19%	24%	22%
USA	2010	S & P 500		18%	38%	34%	10%
Israel	2010	Tel Aviv 100		9%	17%	62%	12%
UK	2010	FTSE 250		2%	10%	36%	52%
Canada	2009	CBI 100		22%	28%	33%	17%
South Africa	2009	JSE 380		18%	21%	28%	33%
UK	2009	FTSE 250		2%	8%	36%	54%
Canada	2008	CBI 100		21%	30%	32%	17%
UK	2008	FTSE 250		3%	6%	36%	56%
Canada	2007	CBI 100		18%	33%	32%	17%
UK	2007	FTSE 250		2%	9%	34%	55%

Refer to notes at the end.
Sources: Authors' research., Refs. [29], [31], [34], [23], [25], [44], [52].

States, Canada, and South Africa are the few countries where more than 15% boards have three or more women (Table 2.4).

Governance Metric International, in its global study of 4200 companies, found that in 2009, 8.2% [16] companies had three or more

Table 2.4. Boards with 3 or More Women from 2009 to 2011

	2011	2010	2009
North America			
Canada	23.0%	20.0%	22.0%
	CSSBI 100	CSSBI 100	CSSBI 100
USA	18.0%	18%	17.0%
	S & P 500	S & P 500	S & P 500
Europe		23.4%	
		Top 300	
France	57.5%	25.0%	7.7%
	CAC 40	EWM 56	GMI 104
Finland	21.4%	37.5%	22.2%
	GMI 28	EWM 6	GMI 27
Netherlands	6.7%	10.0%	3.3%
	GMI 30	GMI 30	GMI 30
Norway	52.0%	83.3%	69.6%
	GMI 25	EWM 6	GMI 23
Sweden	55.0%	68.8%	40.0%
	GMI 40	EWM 16	GMI 50
UK	4.8%	5.2%	5.5%
	GMI 398	GMI 405	GMI 398
Asia			
China	8.0%	5.1%	6.1%
	Korn 100	GMI 78	GMI 66
Hong Kong	6.0%	7.6%	2.0%
	Korn 100	GMI 79	HSI 42
India	1.6%	1.9%	0.0%
	GMI 61	GMI 53	GMI 54
Indonesia	0.0%	0.0%	0.0%
	GMI 23	GMI 17	GMI 15
Israel	11.8%	9.0%	5.9%
	GMI 17	Tel Aviv 100	GMI 17
Malaysia	5.0%	3.7%	0.0%
	Korn 100	GMI 27	GMI 26
Singapore	0.0%	1.3%	1.1%
	STI 30	ALL SGX	ALL SGX
South Korea	0.0%	0.0%	0.0%
	GMI 91	GMI 81	GMI 86

(*Continued*)

Table 2.4. (Continued)			
	2011	**2010**	**2009**
Australia			
Australia	1.0%	2.0%	3.6%
	Korn 100	GMI 200	GMI 111
New Zealand	1.0%	0.0%	0.0%
	Korn 100	GMI 12	GMI 12
Africa			
South Africa	41.6%	35.5%	17.5%
	JSE 339	JSE 335	JSE 380
Refer to notes at the end. *Sources: Authors' research., Refs. [29], [31], [38], [41], [25], [4], [16], [44].*			

women on their boards. In 2011 this number had increased marginally to 8.4% [4]. In Canada, France, South Africa, Malaysia, and China, the number of boards with three or more female directors has increased, but countries like South Korea and Indonesia still do not have any boards with three female representations. While more and more boards have at least one female member, not many boards are actually increasing the number of women directors.

2.5 WOMEN IN THE LEAD

If the presence of women on boards is far from satisfactory, the number of women leading boards is even more disappointing (Table 2.5). According to Governance Metric International, only 2.2% [4] of boards had female chairperson in 2011 (2.1% in 2010 [4] and 2.2% in 2009 [16]). The Nordic Board Index 2010, covering 130 Scandinavian companies, reported only 3% [22] of boards having a chairwoman. Norway, Canada, and Australia have been more proactive in appointed chairwomen, showing an increasing trend since 2009. In 2004 no Canadian board had a women chair; this has changed to 9% currently. There are still no women chair in large companies of Denmark, India, and Singapore.

2.6 BRIDGING THE GAP

A balanced board with the right mix of male and female directors would benefit from the strengths of both sexes. The governments of

Table 2.5. Chairwomen on Boards

Country	2011	2010	2009
Norway	12.0%	10.0%	4.3%
	GMI 25	NBI 70	GMI 23
Canada	9.0%	5.0%	3.0%
	CSSBI 100	CSSBI 100	CSSBI 100
New Zealand	4.0%	0.0%	0.0%
	Korn 100	GMI 12	GMI 12
Australia	4.0%	2.5%	2.7%
	Korn 100	GMI 200	GMI 111
China	4.0%	1.3%	1.5%
	Korn 100	GMI 78	GMI 66
South Africa	3.5%	4.1%	4.6%
	JSE 339	JSE 335	JSE 380
Hong Kong	3.0%	1.3%	1.3%
	Korn 100	GMI 79	GMI 79
Sweden	2.5%	1.0%	2.0%
	GMI 40	NBI 20	GMI 50
USA	2.3%	2.6%	2.0%
	Fortune 1000	Fortune 500	Fortune 500
Malaysia	2.0%	0.0%	0.0%
	Korn 100	GMI 27	GMI 26
Finland	0.0%	5.0%	0.0%
	GMI 28	NBI 20	GMI 27
Israel	0.0%	5.0%	0.0%
	GMI 17	Tel Aviv 100	GMI 17
India	0.0%	3.8%	3.7%
	Sensex 30	GMI 53	GMI 54
Singapore	0.0%	2.7%	3.4%
	STI 30	All SGX	GMI 59
Netherlands	0.0%	0.0%	0.0%
	GMI 30	GMI 30	GMI 30
Denmark	0.0%	0.0%	0.0%
	GMI 24	NBI 20	GMI 26

Refer to notes at the end.
Sources: Authors' research., Refs. [29], [34], [23], [31], [38], [25], [4], [16], [44], [52], [22], [41]

Table 2.6. Targets for Women on Boards

Country	Recommended Female Targets on Boards	Target Year
European Union [53]	30% 40%	2015 2020
Belgium [53]	1/3	2017
Finland [54]	At least one female director	2010
France [53]	20% 40%	2014 2017
Germany	20% 40%	2018 2023
Iceland [55]	40%	2013
Italy [53]	1/3	Renewals after Aug 2011
Netherlands [55]	30%	2016
Norway [56]	40%	2005
Spain [53]	40%	2015
UK [55]	25% 30%	2015 2020
Australia [57]	25%	2014
Malaysia [58]	30%	2016

several countries, particularly in Europe, have recommended and even legislated for quotas of women board members to improve the ratio (Table 2.6). Although this has resulted in a substantial increase in women directors in countries such as Norway, where it is mandatory, it may often result in appointing women for "tokenism." Women appointed just to fulfill a quota may be not of the desired caliber, weakening the quality of the board as a whole. As the supply of women who can be considered for board membership is limited, the same woman may be appointed as a director in many companies. This could destroy the competitive edge of the boards appointing that particular individual. The effective contribution of such an overburdened board member is also questionable.

Companies need to have a more open approach and facilitate opportunities for women to have board roles. Implementing work–life balance measures by allowing flexible working hours and accepting that women need career breaks could go a long way in encouraging women to aspire to senior-level positions. Organizations must strive for gender equality at all levels of the organization and ensure equal

Table 2.7. Women Appointments on Boards

Country	Sample	2011	2010	2009	2008	2007
Canada	CSSBI 100	29.0%	20.0%	13.0%	26.0%	17.0%
Australia	ASX 200	28.0%	25.0%	5.0%	8.0%	8.0%
UK	FTSE 100	22.5 %	13.3%	14.7%	11.0%	20.0%
Netherlands	Euro Next 97	11.5%	11.0%	12.5%	—	
USA	Fortune 1000	8.3%	—	—	—	—
Singapore	All SGX	—	9.0%	6.9%	—	—
Hong Kong	HSI	10.1%	11.2%	12.7%	—	—

Refer to notes at the end.
Sources: Refs. [27], [23], [31], [44], [46], [47], [52], [59], [60].

pay for men and women in similar roles. Insisting on equal male and female nominees when board recruitments are done would give women a fairer chance. This is likely to necessitate actively searching for suitable women, thereby bringing forward women who are not so visible. Appropriate networking and mentoring facilities will help women prepare for top positions. If equal growth and promotion opportunities are facilitated over time, there will be a good number of women at senior positions that can be considered for board-level positions.

Women need to become more visible by attending and speaking at professional gatherings and networking with peers from different industries. To increase the current female proportion on boards to the desired levels of 30% to 40%, companies are appointing more women to their boards (Table 2.7). The percentage of new women appointments as a percentage of total new appointments over the last few years shows that some countries, Canada, Australia, and the UK in particular, are making serious efforts to improve the ratio of women on boards. Surprisingly, American companies are far behind Scandinavian countries in gender diversity on their boards—only 8.3% [23] of new appointments were women.

2.7 TOWARD A BROADER BASE

Companies are facing a huge talent crunch that goes right up to the board level. Currently there are not enough talented male directors who can help boards face the ongoing challenges. Men currently serving on boards are not in a position to take additional responsibility. Continuing reliance on existing directors is likely to dilute the quality of board members. Broadening the talent pool by including women directors will help boards get skilled and competent members with a diversity of perspectives and leadership styles who can significantly contribute to board performance.

NOTES

1. The sample describes the study and the sample size.
2. Figures from different studies, samples, and sample size may not be comparable and may not reflect a true trend.
3. Data in tables are compiled from various sources.

ABBREVIATIONS

ASX	Australian Securities Exchange
ATX	Austrian Traded Index
CSSBI/CBI	Canadian Spenser Stuart Board Index
DAX	Deutscher Aktien Index
EWM	European PWN Board Women Monitor
Fort	Fortune
FP	Financial Post
FT	FTSE
GMI	Governance Metric International
H & S	Hedrick and Struggles
HIS	Hang Seng Index
JSE	Johannesburg Stock Exchange
Korn	Korn/Ferry Institute
NBI	Nordic Board Index
NZSX	New Zealand Stock Exchange
PSI	Portuguese Stock Index
S & P	Standard and Poor
SBI	Sweden Board Index
SGX	Singapore Stock Exchange
STI	Strait Times Index
SMI	Swiss Market Index
WSE	Warsaw Stock Exchange

REFERENCES

[1] Catalyst, Statistical Overview of Women in the Workplace, 2012.

[2] Catalyst, Statistical Overview of Women in the Workplace, Quick takes 2011.

[3] A. McIntyre,Tomorrow's Boards: Creating Balanced and Effective Boards Australian Institute of Company Directors, <http://www.companydirectors.com.au>, 2011.

[4] Governance Metric International Women on Board Report 2011.

[5] Federal Glass Ceiling Commission. Solid Investments: Making Full Use of the Nation's Human Capital. Washington, D.C.: U.S. Department of Labor, November 1995, p. 4.

[6] S.L. Harlan, C.W. Berheide, Barriers To Workplace Advancement Experienced By Women In Low-Paying Occupations United States Glass Ceiling Commission January *Federal Publications*. Paper 122, 1994. iii, <http://digitalcommons.ilr.cornell.edu/key_workplace/122>.

[7] Glass Ceiling Commission - Good for Business: Making Full Use of the Nation's Human Capital U.S. Glass Ceiling Commission 3-1-1995, 8.

[8] A.M. Morrison, The New Leaders: Guidelines on Leadership Diversity in America, Wiley, 1996.

[9] McKinsey report, Women Matter 2, Female Leadership, A competitive edge for the future. 2008.

[10] Think Tank: Marketing to women - The gender factor Peter Crush, Marketing Direct, 31 December 2004 <http://www.brandrepublic.com/news/233078/>.

[11] McKinsey report, Women Matter, A corporate Performance driver, 2007.

[12] R. Sealy, E. Doldor, V. Singh, S. Vinnicombe, Women on Boards October 2011, International Centre for Women Leaders, Cranfield School of Management.

[13] Catalyst, The Bottom Line: Connecting Corporate performance and Gender Diversity, 2004.

[14] Catalyst, The Bottom Line: Corporate performance and women's representation on boards, 2007.

[15] ASX -500, Women Leaders, Research Notes, Reiby Institute, 30th June 2011.

[16] Governance Metric International Women on Board Report 2009.

[17] Hedrick and Struggles, Corporate Governance Report 2007, Raising the Bar.

[18] European PWN Board Women Monitor, 2004.

[19] European PWN Board Women Monitor, 2008.

[20] European Commission, Database on Women and Men in Decision-making in The EU corporate governance framework, Green Paper European Commission, Brussels, 5.4.2011.

[21] A. Gregoric, L. Oxelheim, T. Randøy, S. Thomsen, Corporate Governance as a Source of Competitiveness for Nordic firms, Nordic Innovation Centre, March 2009.

[22] A. Halawi, B. Davidson, Power Matters: A Survey of Gulf Cooperation Council Boards, The National Investor Market Insight, Investment Research, Regional Strategy May 13, 2008.

[23] BWA South African, Women in Leadership Census 2011.

[24] Canadian Spencer Stuart Board Index 2011, 2010,2009, 2008, 2007, 2006, 2005, 2004.

[25] Catalyst Census of Women Board Directors of Canada 2001.

[26] Catalyst Census of Women Board Directors of Fortune 1000, 1999.

[27] Catalyst Census: Fortune 500 Women Board Directors 2011, 2010, 2008, 2006, 2003, 2001.

[28] Catalyst Quick take, Women in U.S. Management 2011.

[29] European PWN Board Women Monitor, 2010.

[30] European PWN Board Women Monitor, 2006.

[31] Hedrick and Struggles, Corporate Governance Report 2011, Challenging Board Performance.

[32] Hedrick and Struggles, Corporate Governance Report 2009, Boards in Turbulent Times.

[33] K. Pajo, J. McGregor, J. Cleland, Profiling the Pioneers: Women Directors on New Zealand's Corporate Boards, Women in Manag. Rev. 12(5) (1997) 174–181. © MCB University Press ISSN 0964-9425.

[34] Korn/Ferry Market Cap 100 report 2010.

[35] A. Yi, Korn/Ferry's Asia Pacific Board Diversity Study, Mind the Gap: Half of Asia's Boards Have Bo Women, a Risky Position for Governance and Growth, 2011.

[36] M. Dieleman, S. Lin, Singapore Board Diversity Report, Gender Diversity in SGX Listed Companies, Centre for Governance, Institutions and Organizations of NUS Business School, Oct 2011.

[37] M. Gamba, A. Goldstein, The gender dimension of business elites: Italian women directors since 1934 Working Paper 27 May 2008 www.econpubblica.unibocconi.it.

[38] Mijntje Lückerath-Rovers inaugurele rede, The Dutch Female Board Index 2011, Nyenrode Business University (Erasmus University Rotterdam).

[39] National Securities and Exchange Commission Annual Report on Corporate Governance 2009.

[40] New Zealand Census of Women Participation 2010.

[41] New Zealand Census of Women Participation 2008, 2006, 2004.

[42] S. Mahtani, K. Vernon, R. Sealy, Women on Boards: Hang Seng Index 2009, Cranfield School of Management, November 2009.

[43] Spencer Stuart Sweden Board Index 2008.

[44] Spenser Stuart, Nordic Board Index 2010.

[45] Spencer Stuart Board Index 2011, 2010, 2009, 2007.

[46] Statistics, Directors resource centre, Australian Institute of Company Directors, <http://www.companydirectors.com.au/Director-Resource-Centre/Governance-and-Director-Issues/Board-Diversity/Statistics>.

[47] The 2010 Israeli Census Report on Women's Representation in Tel Aviv 100 Index Companies, The Catalyst Research Study In Israel.

[48] The Female FTSE Board Report, 2010, 2009, 2008, 2007, 2006, 2005, 2004, 2003, 2002 International Centre for Women Leaders, Cranfield School of Management.

[49] Spenser Stuart, The Netherlands Board Index, 1997, 2002, 2004, 2006, 2008, 2010.

[50] W.G. Simpson, D.A. Carter, F. D'Souza, What do we know about women on boards? J. Appl. Finance 2 (2010) 29.

[51] Corporate Women Directors International 2010 Report: Women Board Directors of the 2009, Fortune Global 200.

[52] CT Partners, Women on Boards: Review & Outlook, 2012.

[53] Deloite, Women in the Boardroom, A global Perspective, November 2011.

[54] New Finnish Corporate Governance Code: Both Genders Represented on the Board, Women on Boards, 8th July 2011 <http://www.europeanpwn.net/index.php?article_id = 713>.

[55] UK Davis Report, Women on boards, February 2011.

[56] Government proposes gender quotas on company boards, June, 2003 <http://www.eurofound.europa.eu/eiro/2003/06/feature/no0306106f.htm>.

[57] Cabinet Approves 30 Per Cent Women as Decision-Makers in Corporate Sector - PM, Office of the Prime Minister of Malaysia, 27.6.2011.

[58] Braund's Churchill Fellowship report, Australia must keep focused to stay ahead on board-room diversity, Women on Board.

[59] A. Banerji, K. Vernon, Standard Chartered Bank, Women on Boards: Hang Seng Index, Community Business March 2012.

[60] Mijntje Lückerath-Rovers inaugurele rede, The Dutch Female Board Index 2010 2009, Nyenrode Business University (Erasmus University Rotterdam).

CHAPTER 3

Gender Diversity—India and Singapore

The impact of women on board performance depends on the number of women on boards and their competencies. This chapter examines the status of women directors in Singapore and India.

3.1 GENDER DIVERSITY

Gender diversity refers to the proportion of females to males in an organizational structure (school, company, courts, etc.) or workplace. The less the difference between the numbers of males and females, the greater is the diversity. Research on social and organizational behavior suggests that heterogeneous teams are more productive. As discussed in earlier chapters, diverse boards with directors with different traits and viewpoints can help in formulating suitable strategies, creative problem solving, and improving productivity, making boards more effective. There is a growing opinion that increasing the number of women on boards has a positive effect on performance, with several countries recommending quotas for women. In this chapter we examine gender diversity in two important Asian countries—India and Singapore.

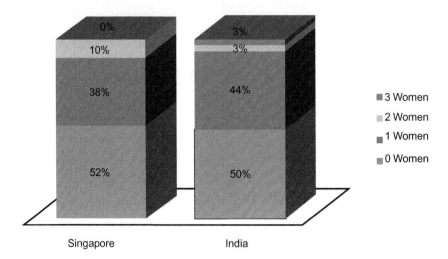

Fig. 3.1. Boards with Women.

3.2 PARTICIPATION OF WOMEN

Singapore, with a female ratio of 5.6%, and India, with 4.8%, have among the lowest proportions of women on boards. In fact, *half of all boards did not have a female director* (Figure 3.1). In India only 3% boards have three women directors, and in Singapore no board has three women directors.

3.3 PASSIVE ROLE OF WOMEN

Where present, women directors appear to have a passive role. Few executive directors are women (2–3%). Women members are mostly independent directors. In India 33% of women are non-executive directors, of whom several are family owners or government/financial companies' nominees (Figure 3.2).

No board has a women chairperson. Only one board in each country has a female chief executive officer. Not only is the number of women directors very small, but on the face of it they do not seem to be making a significant impact on board functioning.

3.4 WOMEN DIRECTORS ARE YOUNGER

Boards consist of men from a wide range of ages, from 39 to 82 and 38 to 89 years, with an average age of 59 and 63 in Singapore and India,

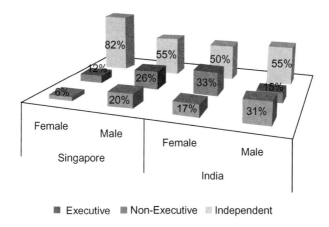

■ Executive   ■ Non-Executive   ▩ Independent

Fig. 3.2. Role of Women on Board.

Table 3.1. Age Profile of Directors				
	Singapore		India	
	Male	Female	Male	Female
Youngest	39	53	38	40
Oldest	82	61	89	75
Spread	43	4	51	35
Average	59	57	63	58

respectively (Table 3.1). In comparison, women's age range is narrower—from only 53 to 61 years in Singapore. With an average age of 57 and 58 in Singapore and India, women directors are much younger than their male counterparts. Until just a few years ago women were not likely to find themselves on boards or senior positions in companies, and this is probably why there are fewer elderly women on boards.

3.5 WOMEN DIRECTORS YET TO GO GLOBAL

Only 7% of the international directors in India are women. Of the 97 international directors in Singapore, none are women. This clearly shows that these two countries are not welcoming of female directors.

3.6 WOMEN: THE NEWCOMERS

The average board tenure of male directors is five years more than female directors in Singapore and three years more in India

Table 3.2. Tenure of Directors				
Board Tenure	Singapore		India	
	Male	Female	Male	Female
Average	7.5 years	2.5 years	8.5 years	5.5 years
Maximum	52 years	6 years	48	15 years
Less than 1 year	14%	18%	3%	6%

(Table 3.2). The gap between the maximum board tenure of male and female directors is very large. Further 3% to 4% more female directors have been a director for less than one year. This clearly indicates that boards are just beginning to include female directors. The statistics show that India has been more favorable than Singapore to the inclusion of women on boards.

3.7 QUALIFICATION MYTH

Contrary to general belief, the graph shows that women are not more qualified than male board members. There are no female doctorates in the boards of either India or Singapore (Figure 3.3). Six percent of women directors in India are undergraduates, a reflection of family-run businesses. In Singapore, however, there are more postgraduate/professional women than men as board members.

As expected, board members come mostly from management background, irrespective of gender (46% in the case of Singaporean female directors) (Figure 3.4). No woman director has an engineering or science background, the second highest category in men. Law was one area where women dominated men. In India the largest portion (29%) of female directors are from the field of economics, something not found on Singapore boards. In Singapore 23% of women are financial professional, 10% more than their male counterparts; in India 6% of women are financial professionals, 11% less than male equivalents. Clearly the education profile is different between the genders.

3.8 LIMITED RANGE OF EXPERIENCE

In comparison to men, 9% more women were from the banking, investment, or financial sector (Figure 3.5). In India most male

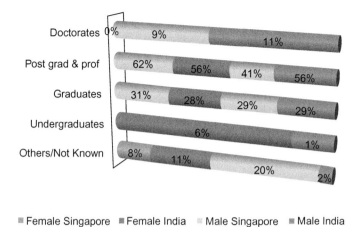

Fig. 3.3. Qualifications of Directors.

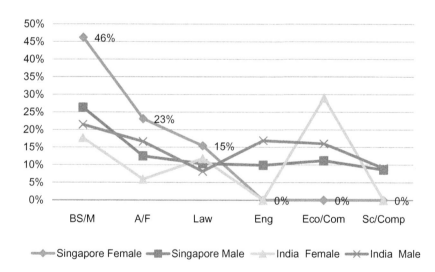

Fig. 3.4. Education Stream of Directors.
Note: Only the highest qualification is considered. Management programs that did not lead to academic qualifications have not been considered.

directors have expertise in a specific sector (42%), whereas a majority of women directors have government and administration experience. Fifteen percent of female directors (only 6% of males) on Singapore boards had expertise in different aspects of the law. There are no women directors with experience in the steel, petroleum, power, or

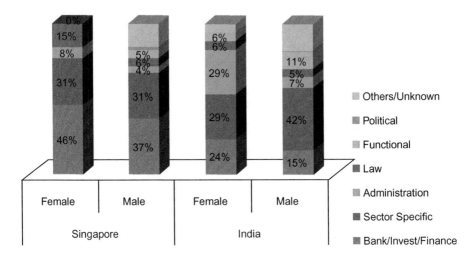

Fig. 3.5. Experience of Directors.
Note: Based on profile. Only one major experience was considered.

shipping and logistics sectors. Some male directors are from a political background, but no female director has a political background. In short, female directors were from select business sectors in terms of both functional and industrial experience.

3.9 WOMEN MATTER

Increasing the number of women on boards may have positive effects due to the diversity of attitudes, attributes, and skills. They are making significant contributions in areas that require expertise in law, banking and finance. Women directors are champions for change because they tend to be younger and newer to the board than their male counterparts. They are relatively more open to new ideas and alternative approaches to doing business.

Table 3.3 ROA of Boards with and without Women	
Boards	**Average ROA**
With women	9.612
Without women	8.518
Note: The above is based on research done by the authors on companies of BSE Sensitive Index of India and Strait Times Index of Singapore in 2011.	

The average return on assets (ROA) of boards with women is higher than those without women. The fact that boards with women representation have performed better suggests that having even one woman on board does make a difference (see Table 3.3).

CHAPTER 4

As Companies Go Global, Boards Must Follow

As companies expand their business to a global scale, boards need to be equipped to deal with it. Having representatives on boards from different countries has thus become the need of the day.

4.1 NATIONALITY DIVERSITY

As companies spread their wings and go global, it is important for the board to have directors representing different nationalities. Boards need to understand the potential risks and rewards of doing business in different countries. Besides the legal and economic environment, a deep understanding of the countries' systems, culture, and work ethos is essential. People's traditions, value systems, and lifestyles have a direct impact on business practices in a country. The board as a team must be able to understand the cultural and business needs of different countries.

India is the only country where McDonald's had to introduce burgers without beef (its trademark product) or pork due to the religious sentiments of Indians (Hindus and Muslims). While McDonald's prides itself on maintaining food items that taste the same in any restaurant across the world, over the years it has varied its menu to accommodate the tastes and cultural sensibilities of residents in countries around the world. Business models, negotiation strategies, organizational structures, and people management—all need to be tailored to the individual country's needs. When entering new countries, boards can benefit from insights of members from that geographical region. American companies that are expanding to Asian and emerging economies need to include directors of different nationalities who can help the board in their pursuit. When selecting international directors, the target countries are very important. India, Japan, and China may all be Asian countries, but they are culturally very different. Similarly, the UK, Germany, and Greece may all be part of Europe, but they follow different business and social practices.

Directors from different nations are likely to have divergent upbringing, childhood experiences, and value systems which impact their perspectives, behavior, and thinking. Indians, for example, with strong family values, are more people oriented, whereas Americans' individualism makes them more goal oriented. Europeans, on the other hand, are less religious and tend to be liberal on controversial issues. The Western view is that time, being scarce, is money. The Eastern view is that time is unlimited and can be used flexibly. Such diverse perspectives and views enhance creativity and lead to innovative problem solving.

Geographically diversifying boards is not without its own problems. The concerns in bringing an international director on board are threefold. First, does a new director understanding the language used in board meetings? At times just knowing the language is not enough, as in case of an American board: Although people coming from India or Singapore may know English, their use or interpretation of words is often different. The second concern is the ability of the foreigner to understand the culture and governance requirements of the country, and the third is the long-distance travel required from their own country to attend meetings several times a year, which consumes money, time, and energy. Over a period of time and with the right guidance, the first two concerns can be addressed. Attending board meetings via videoconferencing could be one way of addressing the third concern.

One meeting in a year could be in the home country of the international directors, which would give other directors a chance to have a firsthand experience of the country in which they are doing or planning to do business.

Geographical diversity measures the global representation of boards. Studies have shown that companies with multinational boards yield better shareholder returns. Boards with national diversity can successfully deliver global integration with local relevance.

4.2 LEVEL OF GLOBAL REPRESENTATION

"In the 1970s, the appointment of an American CEO in the British coal industry provoked howls of protest" [1]. Today Pepsico Inc., an American multinational, is run by Indian-born Indra Nooyi; Tata Motors, a top auto company of India, has a German CEO; and International Airlines, a Spanish company and the parent company of British Airways, is headed by a person from Ireland.

Out of strategic necessity, boards of leading companies have become "importers" of directors. Since 2005, international directors comprised an average of 30% [2] of the annual director appointments in Canada, with 40% [2] of all new directors being international. Fifty-three percent [3] (up from 45% [4] in 2005) of the 200 largest US companies have a non-US director. "One in four large European listed companies has no foreign directors on its board though they have significant revenue streams and operations in other countries" [5] (see Figure 4.1).

In European countries such as France, the UK, and Switzerland, 95% or more companies have at least one international director. A majority of countries have an international director in at least 50% of companies. In Italy and Poland, only 32% and 42% boards have a foreign director.

Only 30% of Indian boards have an international director (Figure 4.2). Only 3% of boards have directors from five different countries. No board has representatives from more than five countries. In the case of Singapore, as many as 24% of the boards have directors only from Singapore and more than three-quarters have at least one international director. At the same time, 28% of Singapore boards

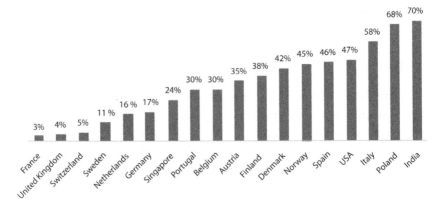

Fig. 4.1. *Proportion of Boards in 2011 with No International Director.* Sources: Refs. [3,6], and authors' own research.

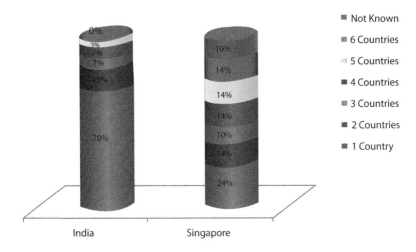

Fig. 4.2. *Level of Globalization.*

have directors representing five or more countries. Singapore boards are more regionally diverse than Indian and US companies, with some boards being more regionally diverse than others.

4.3 GLOBALIZATION ABSENT IN INDIA AND US

In Singapore about one-third of directors are from other countries. In comparison, only 8% [3] of US directors are non-US, up slightly from 6% in 2005 [4]. Thirty-three percent [7] of directors of public companies in Australia were born there. In Europe about 24% [6] of directors are nonnationals, having grown gradually from 14% [8] a decade ago.

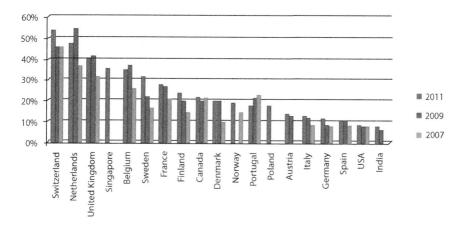

Fig. 4.3. Proportion of International Directors. Sources: Refs. [3,5,6,8–14], and authors' own research.

There are, however, great disparities among European countries. While Switzerland leads the way with 53% [6], only 10% [6] of board members in Spain are nonnationals (see Figure 4.3).

Even in 1998, 16% [15] of UK directors were foreigners, a figure that has risen steadily to 23% [15] in 2001, to 28% in 2004 [16], to the current level of 40% [17]. Of total Canadian directorships, international directors make up about one-fifth (22%) [13], resulting in an average of two international directors per board. In India only 7% of directors are from other countries. This could be because several Indian directors have international education or experience. An additional deterrent could be that the cost of having an American or European director is very high, due to a disadvantageous exchange rate.

4.4 REGIONAL BIAS

Although more than 60% of directors in Singapore are natives, Southeast Asian countries top the list in international directors, with a 13% share. Some of the companies listed on the Singapore stock exchange are based in other countries, particularly Hong Kong, Malaysia, and Indonesia. When comparing directors' country to the country of the company, the share of local directors increased by about 4% (64.6% to 68.2%). Unmistakably, companies prefer local directors to directors from foreign countries. More than 82% of directors on Singapore boards are from Asia. Another 13% were from the United States or UK. Less than 5% come from other parts of the world. In

US companies, of the non-US directors, 17% were born in the UK, 15% in Canada, and 14% in India [3]. This has shown significant change since 2006, when about 50% were from the UK or Canada, 20% from Europe (Germany, France, and the Netherlands), and another 8% from Australia, all Western countries with little representation from Asia [4]. The share of Indians on US boards has doubled since 2007. Understandably, US residents made up 75% [13] of the overall mix in Canada due to its proximity, which embeds similar social and business cultures and reduces traveling costs. The proportion of representation from different regions has remained more or less constant since 2007 (see Table 4.1).

In Australia [7], 10% of directors are from the UK, 3% from New Zealand, 2.8% from the United States, 2.2% from South Africa, and another 15% from 100 different countries. In Europe [6], as expected, of the nonnational directors, 13% come from France, 10% from the UK, 9% from Germany, and 33% from other European countries. That is, almost two-thirds of the international directors are from Europe, 23% from North America, and the balance (12%) from rest of the world. Netherlands boards consist of 22 [18] nationalities, with most foreign directors coming from the United Kingdom, the United States, Belgium, France, and Germany.

The preference for appointing directors from similar countries belonging to same region is obvious in Figure 4.4.

4.5 FORCED GLOBALIZATION

In India only 7% of directors are from other countries. Two percent of directors on Indian boards are from Japan and about 1% each from the United States, UK, Germany, and Singapore. These members are mostly representatives of associated foreign companies which they have taken over or to which they have ties (Table 4.2).

Studies in Nordic countries [19] suggest that foreign ownership is a major thrust for the internationalization of boards. Similarly, in a Russian study it was found that 57% [20] of independent directors in 80% of Russian companies that are listed internationally are foreign nationals, obviously to build confidence within the international community of investors. In contrast, only 22% [20] of Russian companies planning for an initial public offering (IPO) had a few international directors.

Table 4.1. Regional Breakdown of International Directors

Country	Year	North America	Europe	UK	France	Germany	Australia & NZ	Asia	India	South America	ME & Africa	Others
USA [3,9,10]	2011	15%		17%					14%			54%
	2009	17%		20%	9%	8%	7%		9%			30%
	2007	15%		26%	7%	9%	6%		7%			30%
Canada [11–13]	2011	75%	7%	7%			2%	5%		3%	1%	
	2009	74%	8%	6%			3%	4%		5%		
	2007	78%	9%	4%				4%		4%	1%	
Europe [5,6,8]	2011	23%	33%	10%	13%	9%	6%		3%	3%		
	2009	21%	18%	15%	19%	15%	6%		3%	3%		
	2007	20%	30%	12%	14%	12%						12%
India*	2011	18%		11%	7%	14%		43%			7%	
Singapore*	2011	16%	5%	22%			3%	50%		1%	3%	
Australia [7]	2009	8%		30%			9%				7%	45%

Note: Europe excludes UK, France, or Germany where specified.
* Authors' own research.
Sources: Refs. [35–13].

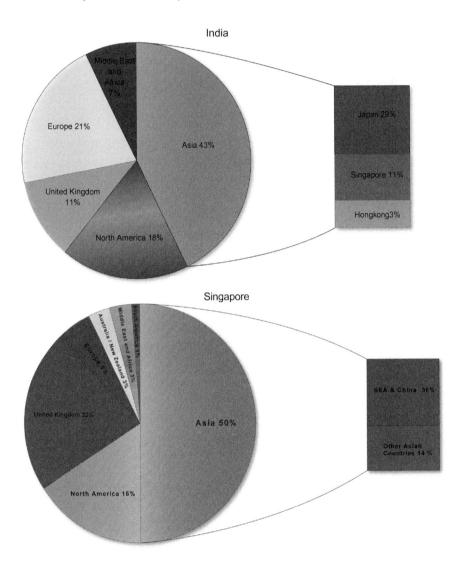

Fig. 4.4. Regional Bias.

4.6 INTERNATIONAL WOMEN DIRECTORS

Only 7% of international directors in India are women. Of the 97 international directors in Singapore, none are women. Asian countries seem to lag in comparison to Europe in appointing foreign women directors. In 2008 almost one-quarter [21] of women directors in Europe were international members. Thirty-six percent [22] of female directors in the Netherlands did not have Dutch nationality, compared to 24% [22]

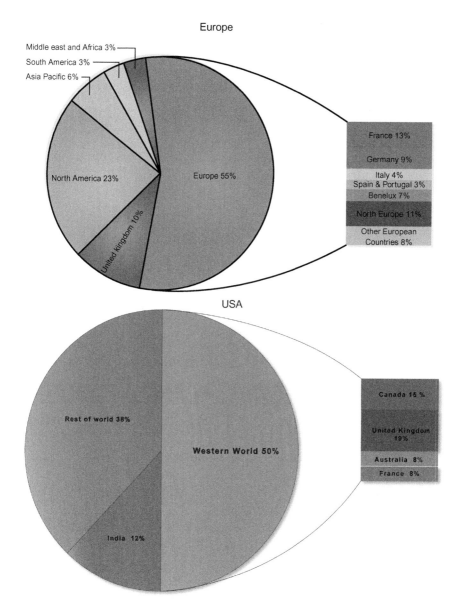

Fig. 4.4. (Continued)

of men. Currently in the UK (see Figure 4.5), about 65% of male directors are British nationals, 12% are EU citizens, and another 11% are from the United States and Canada [17]. Of the women directors, 55% are British, 9% are EU citizens, and as many as 29% of the female directors come from the United States and Canada [17]. The rest of

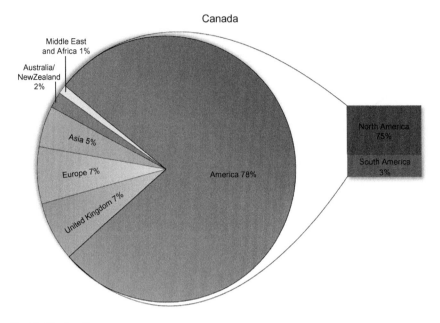

Fig. 4.4. (Continued)

Table 4.2. Ties Force Internationalization

Indian Company	Foreign Company	Country
Bharti Airtel Ltd	Singtel	Singapore
Tata Motors Ltd	Land Rover	Germany
Hero Honda Motors Ltd	Honda	Japan
Maruti Suzuki Ltd	Suzuki	Japan
Tata Steel Ltd	Corus	UK

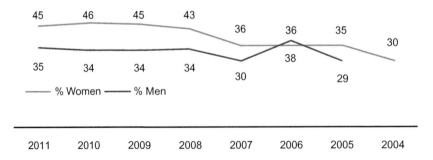

Fig. 4.5. International Directors in the United Kingdom. Source: [23].

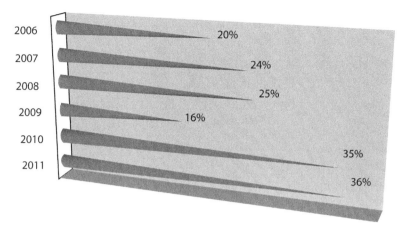

Fig. 4.6. New Women International Directors in Canada. Source: Refs. [2,13].

the women directors come from countries such as Kazakhstan, Saudi Arabia, Zambia, China, and South Africa. In 2004, 70% of women directors were UK nationals, 19% were from the United States, and 7% from Europe; the remainder of this group was from Hong Kong, Australia, and New Zealand [16]. This shows that, over the years, not only has the proportion of international women directors in Britain increased; it has become much more globally diverse.

Since 2007 the increase in women international directors has been much more prominent then that of men. One argument put forth for this is that the UK boards are killing two birds with one stone—fulfilling the need for both nationality and gender diversity at the same time. A similar trend is found in Canada, with 36% [13] of all newly appointed women directors being from outside Canada, up from 20% [11] in 2006 (Figure 4.6). What is surprising, though, is that all of the 36% were US residents.

4.7 SKILL AND TALENT MATTER TO SINGAPORE

Only 45% of executive directors in Singapore are local, 36% are from other Asian countries, and another 15% are from European countries. Of all the Singaporeans on boards, 12% are executives, 20% non-executives, and as many as 68% are independent directors. Thirty-five percent of Asians directors (other than Singaporean) were executive

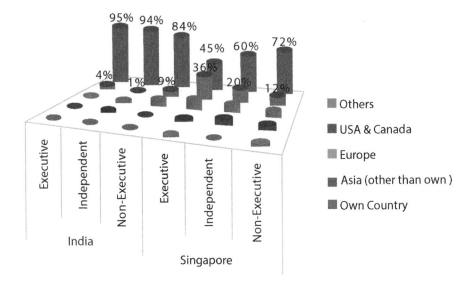

Fig. 4.7. Role of International Directors.

directors. This suggests that in the selection of executive directors, talent and ability to run the company are more important than the country they belong to (Figure 4.7).

Companies are besieged with a huge talent gap that extends all the way up to the boardroom. Companies need talented, experienced, and able directors who have the skills to meet new challenges and add value to the organization. The question arises whether companies widen their search to include international directors to fill this need.

A comparison between directors from home and other countries in Singapore shows that international directors with higher qualifications are given preference—5% and 11% more foreign directors were doctorates or postgraduates, respectively, than local directors (Figure 4.8). Forty-four percent of local directors were graduates, as compared to 27% of foreign directors. In India 7% more international directors held doctorates, but professionals and postgraduates on the board were mostly local.

When it comes to appointment of the top man to run the company, Singapore gives talent and capability to manage the firm

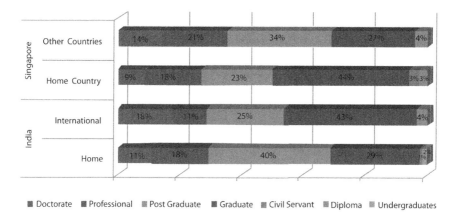

Fig. 4.8. *Qualification vs. Internationalization. Only highest qualification considered.*

priority, as 46% of the CEOs are non-Singaporeans. India Inc. believes in being patriotic, with more than 90% of the CEOs being Indians. The auto industry seems to be the exception, with Maruti Suzuki and Tata Motors having CEOs from Japan and Germany, respectively.

The nature of experience is also a factor in selecting foreign directors. The experiences of directors may be classified into four categories: first, those directly related to business, say marine experience of a board member in companies doing marine business; second, experience closely related to the company's business, such as investment experience for a director in a banking company, or a board member in a company in the resort business who is an architect; third, functional experience like accounting, marketing, and law; and finally, experience that is unrelated, having no obvious link to the nature of the company's business (see Figure 4.9).

In India 71% and in Singapore 37% of international directors have experience directly related to the business of the company. In addition, 40% of foreign directors in Singapore have functional expertise. Local board members with experience not related to company activities are almost double those of international directors. Interestingly, all foreign CEOs had significant expertise in the company's business.

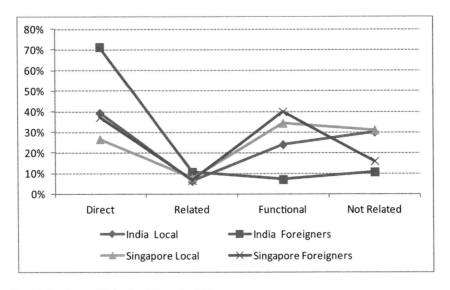

Fig. 4.9. Experience of National and Nonnational Directors.

4.8 INTERNATIONAL DIRECTORS ARE YOUNGER

Board members from foreign countries are younger on average by three years (Table 4.3). In Singapore 15% of local directors are more than 70 years old; in contrast, only 6% of international directors are more than 70 years old, and 16% of international directors were young (less than 50 years), double the local (8%) young directors.

Singapore companies are definitely including international directors to bring more talent and skill on board, in terms of both qualifications and experience. Younger international directors are being appointed who can help the board gear up to face the challenges of the modern world.

4.9 GLOBALIZATION OF BOARDS: IN INFANCY

Directors from the home country had served on the board of the company longer than directors from others countries, with the maximum duration being double in Singapore and six times in India (Table 4.4). Ninety-three percent and 61% of international directors in India and Singapore, respectively, have been on the board for five years or less. On the other hand, only about 50% of directors from the home country have been on the board for five years or less. In India no foreign

Table 4.3. Age of Local and Foreign Directors

Age (in Years)	Home Country	Other Country	Difference
	Singapore		
Minimum	43	39	−4
Maximum	82	74	−8
Range	39	35	−4
Average	60	57	−3
	India		
Minimum	38	47	+7
Maximum	89	81	−6
Range	51	34	−17
Average	63	60	−3

Table 4.4. Tenure of Directors

Duration (in Years)	India		Singapore	
	Home	Others	Home	Others
Average	9	3	7	6
Maximum	48	8	44	22
Less than 1	3%	0%	13%	20%
1−5 years	47%	93%	40%	41%
6−10 years	20%	7%	29%	21%
10−15 years	12%	0%	8%	8%
15−20 years	8%	0%	2%	6%
More than 20	11%	0%	8%	5%

director has been on a board for more than eight years. All this implies a bias in favor of directors from the home country. It also suggests that the globalization of boards has gained prominence only in recent years. Singapore appears to have taken the lead, with 5% of non-Singapore directors being on that board for more than 20 years.

4.10 GLOBALIZATION OF BOARDS GIVEN THUMBS UP

Boards, because of business compulsions, are increasingly including more and more nonnational directors. Nationality diversity is much more common than gender diversity. With the exception of Finland, the United States (which is among the lowest in terms of

Table 4.5. Nationality vs. Gender Diversity

Country	Foreigners	Female	More Globalization
Switzerland	53%	11%	42%
Netherlands	47%	9%	38%
Singapore	35%	6%	29%
Belgium	34%	8%	26%
United Kingdom	40%	14%	26%
France	27%	11%	16%
Portugal	17%	4%	13%
Italy	12%	4%	8%
Poland	15%	8%	7%
Denmark	19%	14%	5%
Austria	13%	8%	5%
Canada	22%	17%	5%
Sweden	31%	27%	4%
India	7%	5%	2%
Spain	10%	9%	1%
Germany	11%	11%	0%
Finland	23%	25%	−2%
USA	8%	16%	−8%
Norway	18%	36%	−18%

Based on Figures 4-1, 2-1, and 2-2.

internationallization), and Norway (which has the highest percentage of women directors), most countries have a higher level of foreign directors on boards than of women (Table 4.5).

What is of concern, however, is that companies tend to take international directors from countries with similar cultures and business environments—Canada from the United States, Singapore from Southeast Asia, and US companies from Western countries—defeating the very objective of regional diversity. Singapore companies have comparatively more regionally diverse boards than most other countries. Their boards may not be global, but they are definitely Asian boards, not just Singaporean boards.

Companies are strengthening their boards with talented and able directors, but from similar cultural backgrounds. International directors with higher qualifications and expertise in the area of the company's business are sought after. Bringing necessary talent and skill to the board definitely is a factor in recruiting international directors.

REFERENCES

[1] E. Marx, 'Route to the Top, a Transatlantic Comparison of Top Business Leaders' 3, http://www.heidrick.com/PublicationsReports/PublicationsReports/RoutetotheTop.pdf.

[2] Canadian Spencer Stuart Board Index, Board Trends and Practices of Leading Canadian Companies 2010.

[3] Spencer Stuart Board Index 2011.

[4] Spencer Stuart Board Index 2006.

[5] Hedrick and Struggles, Corporate Governance Report 2009, Boards in Turbulent Times.

[6] Hedrick and Struggles, Corporate Governance Report 2011, Challenging Board Performance.

[7] Australian Government, Corporation & Market Advisory Committee, Diversity of Board of Directors Report, March 2009.

[8] Hedrick and Struggles, Corporate Governance Report 2007, Raising the Bar.

[9] Spencer Stuart Board Index 2007.

[10] Spencer Stuart Board Index 2009.

[11] Canadian Spencer Stuart Board Index, Board Trends and Practices of Leading Canadian Companies 2007.

[12] Canadian Spencer Stuart Board Index, Board Trends and Practices of Leading Canadian Companies 2009.

[13] Canadian Spencer Stuart Board Index, Board Trends and Practices of Leading Canadian Companies 2011.

[14] India Board Report 2009, Board Composition Effectiveness and best Practices.

[15] V. Singh, S. Vinnicombe, The 2002 Female FTSE Report, Women Directors moving Forward Cranfield Centre for Developing Women Business Leaders, School of Management. Cranfield University.

[16] V. Singh, S. Vinnicombe, The 2004 Female FTSE Report, Cranfield Centre for Developing Women Business Leaders, School of Management. Cranfield University.

[17] R. Sealy, S. Vinnicombe, The Female FTSE Board Report, 2012, International Centre for Women Leaders, Cranfield School of Management.

[18] Spenser Stuart, The 2010 Nordic Board Index.

[19] A. Gregoric, L. Oxelheim, T. Randøy, S. Thomsen, Corporate governance as a source of competitiveness for Nordic firms, March 2009.

[20] Hedrick & Struggles. Russia & CIS Board Insight, "Independent Foreigners" on the Board of Directors of a Russian Company, Importance of a successful overseas IPO.

[21] Third Bi-annual European PWN BoardWomen Monitor 2008, European Professional Women's Network.

[22] Mijntje Lückerath-Rovers inaugurele rede, The Dutch Female Board Index 2011, Nyenrode Business University (Erasmus University Rotterdam).

[23] The Female FTSE Board Report, 2010, 2009, 2008, 2007, 2006, 2005 International Centre for Women Leaders, Cranfield School of Management.

CHAPTER *5*

Board Composition: Veteran or Novice

The length of service of a director on the board has an impact on his/her performance. This chapter illustrates the need for a balance between senior and new directors.

5.1 DIVERSITY OF TENURE ON THE BOARD

Another area that that impacts board effectiveness is directors' tenure. Tenure is the duration for which the director has been a member of the board. Directors who have served on a board for a fair length of time can provide valuable insights based on their thorough knowledge of the company and its business, thereby improving the decision-making process. Awareness of the strengths and weakness of the management and its operations helps in risk mitigation.

An extended board term normally indicates the competence and commitment of board members. Research suggests, however, that such directors often befriend the management at the expense of shareholders. They tend to stick with existing policies and practices and fail to appreciate the need to make changes where required. If members on a board remain constant for a long time, this reduces board conflict, thus improving board dynamics; but on the flip side, there is a risk of excessive cohesiveness and of boards falling prey to groupthink, minimizing diversity of thoughts and ideas, the very purpose of having a team of directors at the helm of affairs.

Long tenures prevent replacement of directors. New directors will offer fresh ideas and perspectives and look at issues from a new angle. Inexperience in their roles and functions as a board member, or unfamiliarity with the company, may initially reduce their positive contributions to the board. Therefore, having a diversity of tenure on the board, with both relatively new and old members, combines the continuity of the board with innovation.

5.2 OPTIMUM TENURE

What should be the length of a board member's term? There are no hard and fast rules for the length of board members' terms. They should be neither too long nor very short. Appointing directors who are likely to serve for only a year or so (say, reaching an age threshold) may not be advisable as there is a learning curve and an orientation period, as in any other job. "Until recently, long tenure was rarely a concern. In fact, it was often a source of pride, particularly for boards with elite membership. Directors joined boards and simply stayed until there was an inciting reason to leave, such as a transaction, a change in management, a change to the corporate structure, or a change in their personal situation" [1]. Having high-profile directors for long periods enhanced corporate image. Dell, eBay, Infosys, and several others have shown that often companies benefit from long tenures of the founding directors, those who had the vision and capability to build the company in the first place. Although the skill and passion of such directors is unquestionable, over time, as business and technology undergo changes, companies may benefit from a change in board membership.

In recent times, the long service of many board directors has often generated passionate debate. Most organizations have a policy that half or one-third of directors will retire by rotation each year. Often the retiring director is only re-elected, defeating the purpose of the rotation. In Switzerland, for example, where election occurs every 2.5 years, average total tenure is still 6.6 years [2]. There have been recommendations from many quarters that the tenure of board directors should be limited (3–9 years). This is similar to most democracies, appreciated in most parts of the world. Elected officials including presidents and prime ministers of countries have fixed terms to ensure a continuous infusion of new ideas through leadership change, while simultaneously preventing abuse of power. This applies equally to board members as leaders of a company. Long continuity on boards, particularly of executive directors, has been the root cause of most frauds and scams.

Many companies limit board members to two or three consecutive terms and require a moratorium of one to five years before a board member may be reappointed. The Institute of Company Secretaries of India (ICSI) has recommended a limited six-year term for independent directors. Such a structural change does not necessarily increase board performance, but it could help eliminate directors whose skill or experience is no longer of use; however, the company may also lose good directors who provide valuable inputs and are assets to the board. An argument against limiting directors' terms is that it does not benefit the decision-making process. New directors do not necessarily imply better directors.

The solution for boards to continuously evolve is not to limit tenure but to have a vibrant election or nomination process that appoints the right candidate to the board. Nomination of directors should be based on a set of appropriate criteria, performance review of directors, and talent gap analysis of the board. While the optimum tenure may be debated, a board should ideally have a mix of directors of different tenures. A board that has directors of diverse tenure will be able to enjoy continuity without stagnation, having the benefits of veteran directors and the advantage of fresh pairs of eyes.

5.3 US AND INDIA BOARDS HAVE MORE VETERANS

Boards in the United States and India have the longest average directors' tenure, at 8.7 and 8.4 years, respectively. Directors in Poland serve on board for the shortest time. In the United States the longest-serving director has a tenure of 62 years [3]; in Singapore it is 52, in India 48, and in Hong Kong 44 years [4]. According to a survey in Australia and New Zealand, the longest duration of a director on a board is only 10 years [5]. While there has been a constant debate around reducing the length of directors' service, since 2009 the average

Table 5.1. Change in Board Tenure

Country	2011	2009	Difference
UK	5.2	4.2	1
Belgium	7.6	6.7	0.9
Italy	5.1	4.2	0.9
Austria	6.6	5.8	0.8
Netherland	5.1	4.3	0.8
Portugal	5.3	4.8	0.5
Denmark	7.2	6.8	0.4
Spain	6.5	6.1	0.4
Switzerland	6.6	6.2	0.4
US	8.7	8.4	0.3
Germany	5.5	5.7	−0.2
France	6.5	6.8	−0.3
Finland	4.6	5.1	−0.5
Sweden	6.1	6.7	−0.6
Poland	3.3		
Norway	4.4		
India	8.4		
Singapore	7		

Sources: Refs. [2,3,6]; [14] and authors' own research.

tenure has increased in most countries, with a few exceptions such as Germany, France, Finland, and Sweden (Table 5.1).

The United Kingdom, with an increase of one year, has shown the maximum rise in tenure, followed by Belgium, Italy, Austria, and the Netherlands. It should be noted that at 4.2 and 4.3 years, the UK, Italy, and the Netherlands had among the lowest average tenures in 2009. Even with an increase of 0.8 to 1 year, their average tenure is on the lower side.

Ninety percent of directors have been on the board for less than 20 years in Singapore and India (Figure 5.1). In Norway 88% of the directors have a tenure of less than eight years; in comparison, only 66% of directors have a tenure of less than eight years in Denmark (Figure 5.2). In the United States 79% of directors have served on the board for less than 10 years. The corresponding figures in Singapore and India are 77% and 68%. Although the United States has the longest average tenure, only 21% of directors serve on the board for more

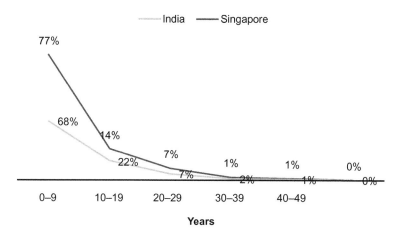

Fig. 5.1. Director Tenure in India and Singapore.

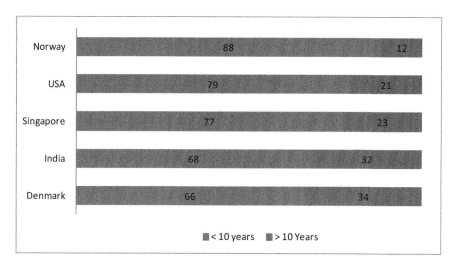

Fig. 5.2. Proportion of Directors with Long and Short Tenure.
Note: For Denmark and Norway the figures correspond for less than and more than eight years. Source: Refs. [3,7] and authors' own research.

than 10 years, indicating that only a select few stay on the board for a very long time.

5.4 INDEPENDENT DIRECTORS HAVE A SHORTER LIFE SPAN

The tenure of independent directors is the shortest, and the tenure of non-executive one phrase non-independent directors is the longest.

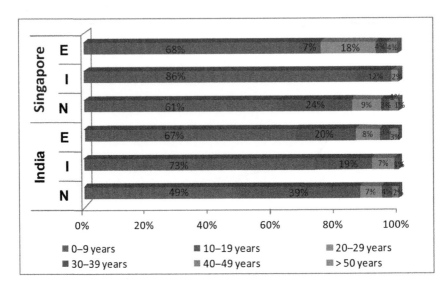

Fig. 5.3. Tenure of Different Directors in India and Singapore.
E = Executive, I = Independent, N = Non-executive non-independent.

More than 90% of independent directors in Singapore and India have a board life of less than 20 years, with 86% in Singapore and 73% in India having tenure of less than 10 years, indicating a high turnover of independent directors (Figure 5.3). On the other hand, 51% of non-executive non-independent directors in India and 39% in Singapore have served on the board for 10 or more years, of which 12%–15% have been on their boards for more than 20 years. This is possibly because promoters/owners are a significant component of non-executive directors, who seem to have an almost perpetual life, with many remaining on the board for 30–40 years, even into their late eighties.

Some 67%–68% of executive directors have a board tenure of less than 10 years. One reason for this could be that companies often have a retirement age for executives, and upon receiving superannuation they must cease to be directors.

If we compare only executive and non-executive directors, the picture looks different (Table 5.2). Executive directors have a longer life than non-executives. The average tenure of non-executive directors is 4.9 in the Netherlands (almost constant since 2008). In India it is has increased over the last two years to eight. In Singapore the tenure of non-executive directors is seven years. The average tenure of executive

Table 5.2. Average Tenure of Executive and Non-Executive Directors

Average Tenure	Netherlands [8]	India[*]	Singapore[*]
Executive director	5.5	9.2	10
Non-executive directors	4.9	8.0	7.0
Difference	0.6	1.2	3.0

[*] Authors' research.
Sources: Ref. [8].

Table 5.3. Average Tenure of Male and Female Directors

Country	Average Male Tenure (Years)	Average Female Tenure (Years)	Women are Newer by (Years)
Netherlands [8]	5.2	4.1	1.1
United Kingdom [10]	5.2	3.5	1.7
Hong Kong [4]	6.5	4.8	1.7
India[*]	8.5	5.5	3
Singapore[*]	7.5	2.5	5

[*] Authors' research.
Sources: Refs. [4,8,10].

directors is much higher. In the Netherlands it is 5.5, up from 4.9 in 2008 [9]; in India it is 9.2, and in Singapore it is as high as 10 years. That is to say, in Singapore, executive directors stay on board three years more than non-executive directors. This distinction results from the fact that, though non-executive non-independent directors have very long tenures, they are comparatively few in number.

5.5 WOMEN—THE NEW ENTRANTS

The average board life of male directors is five years more than that of female directors in Singapore and three years more in India (Table 5.3). In the Netherlands the gap is only one year. The average tenure of women in Singapore is only two and a half years, implying that either women have very recently joined boards in Singapore or the turnover of women directors is very high, the former being more likely.

Table 5.4. Women - the new member on Board							
Board Tenure	Singapore[*]		India[*]		Hong Kong [4]		Australia/ NZ [5]	
	Male	Female	Male	Female	Male	Female	Male	Female
Maximum (years)	52	6	48	15	44	35	10	9
Less than 1 year	14%	18%	3%	6%	–	–	–	–
[*]Authors' research. Sources: Refs. [4,5].								

The gap between the maximum board tenure of male and female directors is very large in most countries (Table 5.4). Three percent to four percent more female directors have been directors for less than one year. This clearly indicates that boards are just beginning to include female directors. Gender discrimination of term of service is not so predominant in Australia and New Zealand.

5.5.1 Women Executives Stay for Longer in India

Differences in tenure are not limited to women and men. Executive male directors are about one and a half years senior to male non-executive directors in the UK, a year in India, and about half a year in the Netherlands, with the gap being less in earlier years (Table 5.5). This follows the general trend seen earlier between executive and non-executive directors. In the UK the difference in length of service of women executive directors was slightly higher than that of non-executive directors in 2011, but showed no difference in previous years. In the Netherlands the trend is the reverse, with the difference in tenure between women executive and non-executive directors decreasing from 2008 to 2011. In India the disparity between women executives and non-executives is very high. A possible explanation is that there are few women at that level in companies, but those that are there, have exceptional capabilities and hence get to be on boards for longer.

A gender comparison between non-executive directors shows that women have a shorter tenure then men by about one to two years. A similar comparison of executive directors reflects that in the UK male

Table 5.5. Gender Bias among Executive and Non-Executive Directors

Tenure		United Kingdom [11,14]			Netherlands [8,9,12,13]			India[*]		
		M	W	Diff	M	W	Diff	M	W	Diff
2011	Executive	6.2	4.1	2.1	5.5	5.4	0.1	9.2	9.3	−0.1
	Non-executive	4.7	3.4	1.3	5	3.8	1.2	8.2	4.7	3.5
	Difference	1.5	0.7		0.5	1.6		1	4.6	
2010	Executive	6.4	4	2.4	5.3	5.5	−0.2	4.1	5.6	−1.5
	Non-executive	4.8	4.1	0.7	5.1	3.6	1.5	4.8	3.7	1.1
	Difference	1.6	−0.1		0.2	1.9		−0.7	1.9	
2009	Executive	5.7	3.7	2	4.7	5.7	−1			
	Non-executive	4.6	3.7	0.9	4.8	3.3	1.5			
	Difference	1.1	0		−0.1	2.4				
2008	Executive	5.6	3.6	2	4.9	6	−1.1			
	Non-executive	4.5	3.5	1	5.1	3.7	1.4			
	Difference	1.1	0.1		−0.2	2.3				

[*]Authors' research.
Sources: Refs. [8,9,11−14].

executive directors are about two years senior to female directors. In the Netherlands and India, on the other hand, executive women directors were about a year senior to their male members earlier, but the gap is now negligible.

5.6 DEGREE OF DIVERSITY

Diversity of tenure is measured by range, that is, Maximum duration − Minimum duration. A high range implies that the board has directors who have been on the board for a long time as well as newcomers.

In Singapore the average tenure range was 17 years (Table 5.6). A variance of 178.22 shows that on some boards directors have around the same tenure (minimum tenure range is 6, excluding the new company with tenure of 0 year), whereas on other boards there are directors with less than one year and those who have been on the board for 40 to 50 years. Similarly, in India the average range of tenure was 22 years with a variance of 154.3, a minimum range of 4, and a

Table 5.6. Degree of Tenure Diversity		
Range of Tenure	India	Singapore
Min	4	0
Max	45	52
Average	22.10	17.31
Median	20	13
Mode	29	13
Variance	154.30	178.22
Standard deviation	12.42	13.35
Kurtosis	−1.03	0.79
Skewness	0.20	1.23
Range	41	52
Count	30	29
Total	375	302

maximum of 45. In both of these countries, with the exception of few cases, boards consist of directors with different tenure.

5.7 NOVICE AND VETERAN

Women have been on boards for a shorter time than men. As seen earlier, international directors have a much shorter tenure than directors from the home country This not only shows a bias in favor of men and local directors; it indicates that gender and geographical diversity have a long way to go.

Companies in India and the United States should take appropriate steps to reduce board tenure. Boards need to consider what the optimum range of tenure for members should be, given the benefits and risks of lengthy director tenure, as well as the limitations of very short tenure based on the needs of the company and the business environment. Length of board tenure must be considered as one parameter for board effectiveness.

A balanced board with the right mix of directors with different tenures will able to benefit from the experience of those who have been on the board for a long time as well as the enthusiasm and new perspectives of rookies. Both India and Singapore have fairly diverse corporate boards in terms of tenure, having a mix of novices and veterans on boards.

REFERENCES

[1] J. Canavan, B. Jones, M.J. Potter, Board tenure: How long is too long? DIRECTORS & BOARDS BOARD GUIDELINES p 39 <http://www.hrsurveysolutions.com/uploads/Board_Tenure__2004_D_B_.pdf>.

[2] Hedrick and Struggles, Corporate Governance Report 2011, Challenging Board Performance.

[3] Spencer Stuart Board Index 2011.

[4] A. Banerji, K. Vernon, Charted Standard Bank Women on Boards: Hang Seng Index 2012, Community Business, March 2012.

[5] B. Groysberg, D. Bell, Australia and New Zealand Board of Directors Survey 2012, Hedrick and Struggles.

[6] Hedrick and Struggles, Corporate Governance Report 2009, Boards in Turbulent Times.

[7] Spenser Stuart, The 2010 Nordic Board Index.

[8] Mijntje Lückerath-Rovers inaugurele rede, The Dutch Female Board Index 2011, Nyenrode Business University (Erasmus University Rotterdam).

[9] Mijntje Lückerath-Rovers The Dutch 'Female Board Index' 2008, Eerasmus Institute Monitoring & Compliance, Erasmus University Rotterdam.

[10] R. Sealy, S. Vinnicombe, The Female FTSE Board Report, 2012, International Centre for Women Leaders, Cranfield School of Management.

[11] The Female FTSE Board Report, 2010, 2009, 2008 International Centre for Women Leaders, Cranfield School of Management.

[12] Mijntje Lückerath-Rovers The Dutch 'Female Board Index', 2009 Eerasmus Institute Monitoring & Compliance, Erasmus University Rotterdam.

[13] Mijntje Lückerath-Rovers The Dutch 'Female Board Index' 2010 Eerasmus Institute Monitoring & Compliance, Erasmus University Rotterdam.

[14] Spenser Stuart Board Index 2009.

CHAPTER 6

Age Diversity—Toward a Balanced Board

The age of directors plays an important role in the way they think and respond to challenges. This chapter takes a look at age diversity on boards.

6.1 WHY AGE DIVERSITY?

Age diversity suggests that board should have a mix of directors of different ages. Traditionally, corporate boards consist of middle- or senior-aged directors. Often a large proportion of the board is formed of retired-age members. The rapid transformations in technology and social trends that companies face call for younger directors who can keep pace with these changes.

Young directors are likely to be more agile, energetic, and supportive of innovation (Figure 6.1). Their risk appetite for new ventures and approaches is likely to be greater. Younger generations have a much better appreciation of the benefits and perils of the latest technology, online applications, and social media. They are able to better understand complex concepts like derivatives or value at risk, which require comprehending intricate mathematical models.

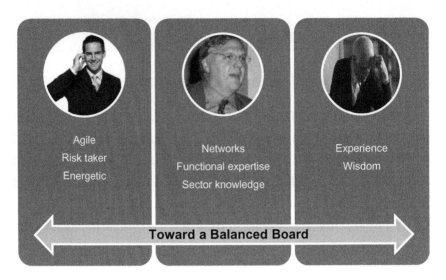

Agile
Risk taker
Energetic

Networks
Functional expertise
Sector knowledge

Experience
Wisdom

Toward a Balanced Board

Fig. 6.1. Age Diversity: Toward a Balanced Board.

Older directors bring experience and wisdom to the board. They are able to take a more holistic approach. Middle-age directors bring to board sectoral and functional expertise. They are in a strong position to take responsibility due to their vast knowledge and experience. A primary responsibility of boards is to acquire resources and develop relationships with external agencies. Senior members, with their strong personal networks, can play a pivotal role in this process.

Age diversity also allows for an easier transition when people retire from the board, as having a range of ages makes it less likely that a large proportion of the members will be retiring at once. It thereby ensures that there will be a sufficient number of experienced board members at any point in time.

Another argument in favor of a board with directors of different age spread is that they will be able to relate better with different stakeholders of varied age groups. Senior members may be more apt to deal with government authorities or regulators. Younger directors may align with the aspirations of the next generation of customers.

Boards of different age groups will have different perspectives and skills that will help create a balanced board. It is important that one age group does not dominate a board's decision-making process; in

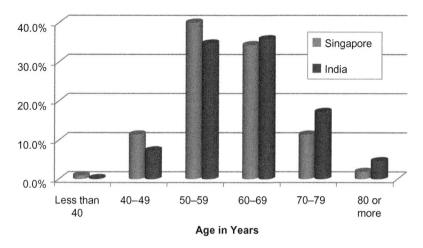

Fig. 6.2. Age Comparison between India and Singapore.

particular, the younger members must participate independently and not be intimidated by their senior counterparts.

6.2 AGE DIVERSITY ON BOARDS

The age diversity of boards in different regions is described with special focus to two Asian economies, India and Singapore.

6.2.1 50s and 60s Rule

The average age of directors in Europe is 58 [4], having decreased slightly since 2009. Within the eurozone one can see a wide range, from 54 in Poland [4] to more than 62 in the Netherlands [4]. Eighty percent of Nordic directors are in the 50−70 age group [9]. In the United States, with 37% of the directors being 64 or over, the average age has been increasing over the last decade [8]. In Australia the average age is 53 [2]; 29% are 60 or over, 32 percent are between 50 and 60, and only 12% are under their 40s [2]. In India the average age is 63, with 70% of the directors being in their 50s or 60s (Figure 6.2). More than 20% of Indian directors are 70 years or over. Whereas hardly any director is less than 40, India can boast of having a nonagenarian on board.

In Sweden almost 80% [7] of directors are between 50 and 70 years, with practically no director being over 70 years old. In Singapore the

Table 6.1. Degree of Age Diversity		
Age	Singapore	India
Youngest director	39	38
Oldest director	82	89
Spread	43	51
Average	59	63
Midpoint	58	62
Norm	64	58
Variance	75	94
Number	105	366
Sample	STI	Sensex

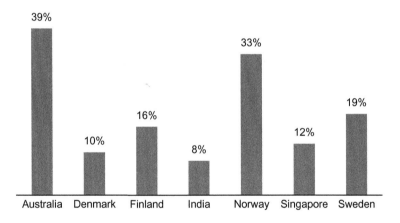

Fig. 6.3. Proportion of Directors Younger Than 50 Years.
Notes: Year of data is as follows: India 2011; Singapore 2010−11; Sweden, Norway, Denmark, and Finland 2010; and Australia 2009.

average age is 59, with 4.6% of directors being more than 80 years old and the youngest being 39. The spread and variance in age distribution is greater in India compared to Singapore (Table 6.1).

Directors in India are among oldest, and directors in Australia are among the youngest. Indian directors are older than directors in Singapore by four years, older than European directors by five years, and older than Australian directors by 10 years.

Australia has the maximum number of directors less than 50 (39%), followed by Norway (33%); India has the least at 8% (Figure 6.3). Although the average age of directors in Europe has fallen, Germany

Table 6.2. Average Age of Directors in European Countries

Country	2011	2009
Europe	58.4	59.0
Austria	56.7	55.9
Belgium	57.8	57.6
Denmark	57.6	56.9
Finland	57.1	56.7
France	60.4	61.6
Germany	57.8	60.1
Italy	59.8	59.6
Netherland	62.4	62.4
Portugal	57.3	55.9
Spain	59.8	58.9
Sweden	55.5	57.1
Switzerland	60.2	59.5

Source: Hedrick and Struggles, Corporate Governance Report 2011, 2009.

(2.3 years), Sweden (1.6 years) and France (1.2 years) are the only countries with a fall in average board age (Table 6.2). In all other countries there has been a slight upward trend.

6.2.2 Young Directors More Active

The average age of executive directors is 57 in India, 55 in Singapore, and 52 in the Netherlands; that of non-executive directors is 63 in India, 59 in Singapore, and 61 in the Netherlands (Figures 6.4 and 6.5). Young board members have a more active role in India, with 67% of directors in their 40s being executive directors. Independent directors are mostly over 60 years. The average age of independent directors in India is 65.4, 61.1 in Singapore, and 62.4 in the United States [8]. This reflects the current scenario where executives on retirement become independent directors. In Singapore there were only two directors over the age of 80, both non-executive directors.

6.2.3 Energetic CEO and Wise Chairperson

The fact that young directors play a more active role is reflected in the age profile of chief executive officers (CEOs). The average age of CEOs is about 54.5 in Singapore, 56.4 in India, and 56.5 in the United States [8] (Table 6.3). Ming Z. Mei of Global Logistic Properties, at 39, is the young CEO in Singapore. The oldest CEO in Singapore is

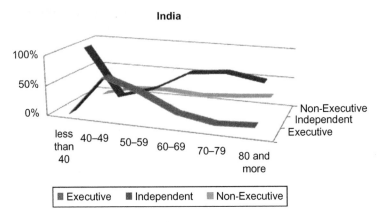

Fig. 6.4. *Average Age of Different Directors in India.*
Note: Non-Executive implies Non-executive non-independent.

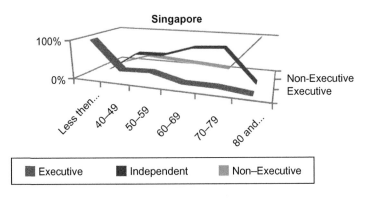

Fig. 6.5. *Average Age of Different Directors in Singapore.*
Note: Non-Executive implies Non-executive non-independent.

Table 6.3. Young CEOs and Old Chairmen			
Region	India[1]	Singapore[1]	Nordic Countries[2]
Average age of director (years)	63	59	56
Average age of CEO (years)	56	55	–
CEO younger by (years)	7	4	–
Average age of chairman (years)	66	66	61
Chairman elder by (years)	3	7	5
Sources: [1] *Authors Own Research.* [2] *Spenser Stuart. The 2010 Nordic Board Index.*			

only 64. Dr. Y. K. Hamied, chairman and managing director of Cipla Ltd., at 75, is the oldest in India.

The average age of board chairs in Nordic countries is 61 [9], much above the directors' average of 56 [9]. In India the average age of chairpersons is 66, three years more than the average board age. Naveen Jindal, chairman and managing director of Jindal Steel and Power Ltd., at 41, is the youngest and Brijmohan Lall Munjal of Hero Honda Motors Ltd. and Keshub Mahindra of Mahindra & Mahindra Ltd. are the oldest, at almost 90. In Singapore the age of board chairs, at 66, is seven years more than the board age, with some being more than 80 years old. Seniority and maturity are given prime importance when choosing chairpersons.

6.2.4 Younger Directors Being Appointed

Boards are appointing younger directors, but the average board age is not changing (Table 6.4). This is possibly because the number of new directors as a percentage of total directors is not substantial and existing directors continue to get older. Newly-appointed directors are about five years younger than the average board in India, the Netherlands, and the United States (India 62.5−57.2; US only independent directors, 62.4−56.7 [8]; Netherlands 57.9−53.5 [5]). In Europe new directors are 3.5 years younger than the average age of directors (58.4−54.9 [4]). In Singapore new directors are younger by only two years, as the average age is lower (59.3−57.5).

Table 6.4. Gap between Age of New Directors and Board Age	
Less Than 4 Years	4 Years or More
Belgium	Austria
Germany	Denmark
Norway	France
Poland	Finland
Portugal	India
Spain	Italy
Singapore	Netherlands
Sweden	United States
Switzerland	
United Kingdom	

Sources: Hedrick and Struggles, Corporate Governance Report 2011, Challenging Board Performance, Spencer Stuart Board Index, 2011 and authors' own research Table 6-4.

Table 6.5. Age of Men and Women Directors

Country	Average age of Women Directors	Average Age of Male Directors	Women are Younger by
Netherlands[1]	53	58	5
UK[2]	55	58	3
Hong Kong[3]	57	60	3
India[4]	58	63	5
Singapore[4]	57	59	2

Sources:
[1] *Mijntje Lückerath-Rovers inaugurele rede, The Dutch Female Board Index 2011, Nyenrode Business University (Erasmus University Rotterdam).*
[2] *Ruth Sealy and Susan Vinnicombe, The Female FTSE Board Report, 2012, International Centre for Women Leaders, Cranfield School of Management.*
[3] *Aparna Banerji and Kate Vernon, Charted Standard Bank Women on Boards: Hang Seng Index 2012, Community Business, March 2012.*
[4] *Authors own Research.*

The average age of directors in countries such as Sweden, Norway, and Poland is already low, so the gap between new directors and board age is not likely to be much. In contrast, the average age in India, France, and the United States is greater, so when young directors are appointed the difference becomes large.

6.2.5 Men Are Older

Women directors are younger than their male counterparts (Table 6.5). In India and the Netherlands, the age gap between genders is more prominent than in the UK, Hong Kong, and Singapore.

Until a few years back, women were not likely to find themselves on boards or in senior positions in companies, which is probably one reason there are fewer elderly women on boards. A majority (87% [5]) of Dutch women directors are younger than 60 years; for the male directors the figure is only 45%. Further, when directors are appointed for the first time, then women are younger than men. In Australia new female directors are aged about 38 and men 41 [2]. In the Netherlands the age of newly-appointed directors in the case of women is 49; for men the figure is 54 [5]. Further, clusters of men in their 70s—and even in some cases octogenarians—in countries like Hong Kong and India further enhances the gap. In India only 41% of women directors are under 60. This is probably a reflection of the culture of family-run businesses in India, where wives (often having large share holdings) are "put" on boards.

Table 6.6. Age of Men and Women Executive and Non-Executive Directors

Country	Executive Directors			Non Executive Director		
	Male	Female	Difference	Male	Female	Difference
Hong Kong[1]	56.1	57.6	−1.5	62.2	56.8	5.4
India[2]	57.1	49.7	7.4	64.7	60.6	4.1
Netherlands[3]	52.2	48.5	3.7	62.0	54.0	8.0
Singapore[2]	54.5	53.0	1.5	60.4	59.0	1.4
UK[4]	52.4	51.7	0.7	60.7	55.5	5.2

Sources:

[1] *Aparna Banerji and Kate Vernon, Charted Standard Bank Women on Boards: Hang Seng Index 2012, Community Business, March 2012.*
[2] *Authors' Own Research.*
[3] *Mijntje Lückerath-Rovers inaugurele rede, The Dutch Female Board Index 2011, Nyenrode Business University (Erasmus University Rotterdam).*
[4] *Ruth Sealy and Susan Vinnicombe, The Female FTSE Board Report, 2012, International Centre for Women leaders, Cranfield School of Management.*

The average age of executive women directors is younger than that of male executive directors by two to three years, with the difference in India being as much as 7.4 years (Table 6.6). Hong Kong is the only country where women executive directors are older than their male counterparts. Non-executive male directors are older than women by about four to five years, with the difference in the Netherlands being as high as 8 years. The difference in age of women and men non-executive directors in Singapore is not great.

6.2.6 Age vs Qualifications

In India qualifications of directors in general decrease with increasing age, with some of the very senior directors being undergraduates. Sixty-seven percent of young directors (40−49) are postgraduates in both India and Singapore (Figure 6.6). This drops to 52% (India) and 45% (Singapore) for elderly directors (70−79). The only exception is that 17% of Indian directors in the 70−79 age group have doctorates. Arguably, these are highly skilled and specialized people who are worth retaining on board irrespective of age.

6.2.7 International Directors—Neither Kids nor Grandfathers

Directors from other countries are neither too young nor too old. International members are mostly in their 50s or 60s (Figure 6.7). In Singapore the international director under 40 years is from China. In India Osamu Suzuki (81 years old) from Japan is on the board of Maruti Suzuki India Ltd.

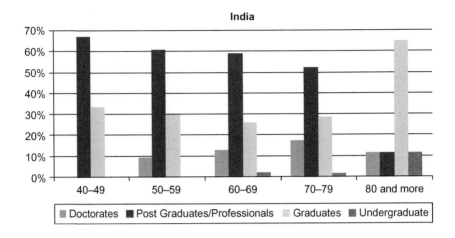

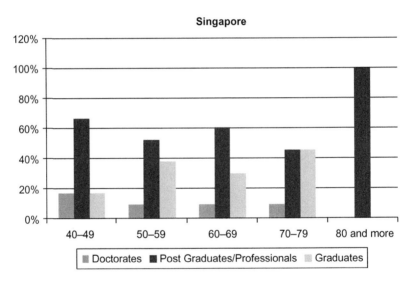

Fig. 6.6. Age vs Qualifications.

6.3 IMPORTANCE OF AGE UNDERMINED

Many companies fail to appreciate the importance of the age profile of their directors. Information on directors' age is available for 72% [4] of European boards. In Singapore and India only about one-third of companies disclose information on the age of directors in either their annual reports or their website. In the UK information of age was available for 97% [6] of directors.

International Directors

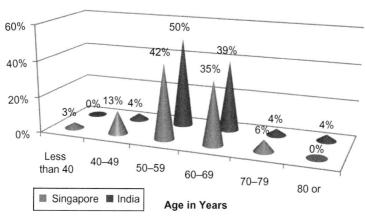

Fig. 6.7. Age of International Directors.

REFERENCES

[1] Aparna Banerji and Kate Vernon, Charted Standard Bank Women on Boards: Hang Seng Index 2012, Community Business, March 2012.

[2] Australian Government, Corporation & Market Advisory Committee, Diversity of Board of Directors Report, March 2009.

[3] Hedrick & Struggles, Corporate Governance Report 2009, Boards in Turbulent Times.

[4] Hedrick & Struggles, Corporate Governance Report 2011, Challenging Board Performance.

[5] Mijntje Lückerath-Rovers inaugurele rede, The Dutch Female Board Index 2011, Nyenrode Business University (Erasmus University Rotterdam).

[6] Ruth Sealy & Susan Vinnicombe, The Female FTSE Board Report, 2012, International Centre for Women Leaders, Cranfield School of Management.

[7] Spenser Stuart, 2008 Sweden Board Index.

[8] Spencer Stuart Board Index, 2011.

[9] Spenser Stuart, The 2010 Nordic Board Index.

CHAPTER 7

Skill Diversity

This chapter discusses the varied skills and experiences needed to be able to perform in the trying times faced by boards under complex global conditions.

7.1 VARIED TALENT

As business becomes more complex and competitive, it is important for board members to have a variety of skills and expertise. This could be functional, industry specific, or specialized expertise (Table 7.1).

Functional: Functional skills relate to the major functions in an organization—finance, accounting, marketing, operations, human resources, and so on. Raising funds, audit committee activities, financial planning and budgeting require inputs from directors who have the relevant financial understanding and experience. Directors with an understanding of human resources (HR) will be able to build a culture that brings out the best in employees. However, most boards generally do not have a HR expert on board. Directors with HR expertise are present in only about 13% of the 30 Sensex companies in India, 3% of the STI companies of Singapore, and in less than 1% [1] of the FTSE 50's boards of directors in the UK. Members with legal backgrounds are able to guide the board in compliance and regulation aspects. In Europe [2] and Singapore 72% boards and in India almost two-thirds of all boards have at least one board member with a legal background, indicating that boards realize the need to include a legal expert.

Table 7.1. Skill Diversity

Functional	Industry	Specialization	Company Profile
• Finanace • Accounting • Human resources • Law • Marketing • Operations	• Oil and gas • Basic materials—chemicals, paper, metals and mining • Industry goods and services • Consumer goods—food, electronics, automobilies, personal goods • Services—media, health care, retail, telecommincations • Banking, insurance, and financial sector • Real estate • Technology • Utilities—power, water	• Intellectual • Branding • Merger and acquisitions • Capital markets • Research	• Big vs small • Private vs government • Listed vs nonlisted • New vs established • Foreign vs national • Global vs local Operations/markets
Note: List is suggestive, not exhaustive.			

Members with different functional expertise should be selected based on the requirements of the company.

Industry specific: If a board member has been involved for a long time with a specific sector—steel, pharmaceuticals, or airlines, for example—he or she is likely to have developed expertise in that sector. Directors with specific training would also be able to contribute significantly to a particular industry—for instance, doctors in the health sector, actuaries in insurance companies, and marine engineers in the shipping industry.

Specialized: Expertise in a particular domain such as capital markets, intellectual property, or mergers and acquisitions are examples of specialized knowledge. An expert in brand management in a FMCG company or an authority on research in a biotech company might prove to be a very useful board member.

Company profile: Directors will have different board experiences in small companies than in big multinationals, in a new company as opposed to a well-established one, a private company as opposed to a publicly listed company, and a government-sponsored organization as opposed to a nongovernmental company. A start-up company may benefit by having board members with entrepreneurial skills. If a company is planning to go public it may be useful to have a few board members with experience in public limited companies.

Boards can improve the quality of their deliberations and decision making with the right combination of directors' expertise profiles.

Knowledge and understanding are built by a combination of education and work experience. Research suggests that multidisciplinary and cross-functional teams solve problems faster and more effectively than teams of like-minded people. Members with a varied of experience—functional, industry-specific, and specialized skills—look at problems differently and focus on different aspects of any issue under consideration. This leads to creative problem solving and innovation decision making.

7.2 PROS AND CONS

With increased global competition, companies put in place cross-functional teams with different backgrounds to solve complex problems, innovate new products and services, reduce costs, and improve quality. Research suggests that members from diverse educational and experiential backgrounds lead to better strategic decision making and tend to outperform groups with members from homogenous backgrounds. A team of engineers will arrive at inferior solutions, and arrive at them more slowly, than if the team has a mix of engineers, finance professionals, lawyers, and industrialists. There is research evidence that diversity within top management teams in terms of education and functional backgrounds has a positive effect on firms in terms of market share and profits.

Teams with a wide range of skills and experience are being employed at all levels of the organization, as they are expected to achieve better results than teams consisting of members with similar expertise. Such diversity can, however, have a negative effect on performance. This is predominantly due to poor communication among team members. Communicating effectively with teammates who do not share a common technical language or perspective is a challenge. Often the question of status can create conflict. Effective management of diversity in boards is necessary to achieve expected performance. Coordination is required to increase group cohesiveness and improve the flow of communication, and greater expenditures may be required for these initiatives.

7.3 FINANCE BACKGROUND IN DEMAND

Since the passing of corporate governance codes, audit committees require the presence of directors who understand financial numbers. In

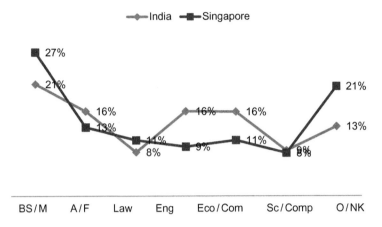

Fig. 7.1. Education Profile of Boards.
Notes: BS/M—Business studies or management; A/F—Accounting or finance; Eng—Engineering; Eco/Com—Economics or commerce; Sc/Comp—Science or computers.

Europe 72% [2] of audit committees have at least one accounting expert (CFO or chartered accountant), up from 63% [3] in 2009. Almost all audit committees in Canada have a financial expert. In several countries such as the United States and India it is mandatory for audit committees chairperson or at least some members to have a financial background. Directors with financial backgrounds represented more than half (58% [4]) of all newly appointed directors, up from 35% [5] a decade ago. In 2006 24% [6] of all new independent directors in the United States were from a financial background. This has fallen to 18% [6] in 2011, indicating that boards now have sufficient members with financial expertise. In India 16% of directors have a finance/accounting degree and 19% have experience in investment, banking, or financial services (see Figures 7.1 and 7.2). Similarly, in Singapore 13% have an education in accounting and 37% have experience in the financial sector. Women directors come largely from a financial background. In India 24%, in Singapore 46%, and in the UK 57% [7] of new appointments among women have experience in finance.

7.4 NEED FOR GENERALISTS

Although diversity of skill is a must, there is also a need for some directors who have general management experience. Non-executive directors, preferably independent directors who have experience as chief executive officers (CEO), would be valuable assets to a board. They

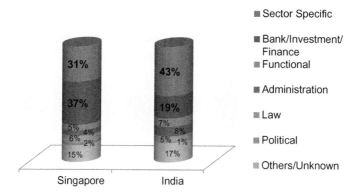

- Sector Specific
- Bank/Investment/ Finance
- Functional
- Administration
- Law
- Political
- Others/Unknown

Fig. 7.2. Experience Profile of Boards.

would understand the problems of the CEO, guide him or her when required, and even challenge the CEO if needed. In Europe about 43% [2] of directors are CEOs or former CEOs. In the United States the proportion of CEOs, COOs, chairmen, presidents, and vice-chairmen among new independent directors is 43% [6], down from 59% [6] a decade ago. Preference is given to retired CEOs more than active ones, as they will be able to devote more time to board activities. Forty-two percent [4] of all new appointments to boards in Canada have CEO experience, 52% [4] of whom were retired. This is about 25% lower than the 57% [8] in 2005. In France, the Netherlands, and Sweden over 60% [2] of board directors have a CEO background; in Denmark, Finland, Switzerland, and the UK a majority of board directors are CEOs; at the opposite end of the spectrum, Poland, Spain, and Portugal have less than a quarter [2] of board directors with experience as CEOs.

Management graduates are much sought after as they have an overall understanding of business needs. A study of Nordic countries [9] found that about 35−50% of members have an education in business or economics. In India 21% and in Singapore 27% of directors have an educational background in business studies or management. In addition, many directors have attended advanced management programs at Harvard or other reputable business schools.

7.5 INDUSTRY EXPERT PREFERRED

The expertise of directors can be classified into four categories in terms of relevance to company business: first, experience directly related to

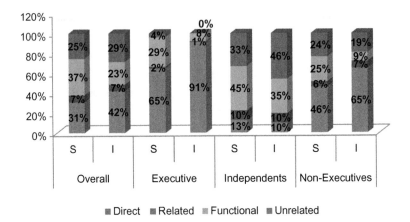

Fig. 7.3. Experience of Directors.
S = Singapore, I = India.

the business, say marine experience in companies doing marine business; second, experience that is closely associated to the company's business, such as an investment analyst or portfolio manager as director in a banking company, an architect in the resort industry; third, functional skills such as accounting, marketing, and law; and finally, unrelated experience, having no obvious link to the nature of company's business (Figure 7.3).

Overall, there appears to be a blend of directors with different experience. On closer examination it is found that 91% of executive directors are industry experts, having experience directly aligned with the company business. This is predominantly because most of them have been working in the same industry, in many cases in the same company, for many years, often as the promoters/owners. In Singapore only about 4% of executive directors have unrelated experience, whereas in India no executive director has unrelated experience. Of the total non-executive directors, about 75% to 80% have experience allied to the company business, or functional skills. On the other hand, only 10−13% of independent directors have expertise directly linked with the company business, but another 10% did have related experience. Thirty-three percent of independent directors in Singapore and 46% in India have unrelated experience. It is evident that industry experts who have an understanding and knowledge of the company business are preferred for the role of executive director. On the other hand, when appointing independent directors, those with diverse and unrelated backgrounds are selected.

It is argued that independent directors who are industry experts can add substantial value to strategic and operational decision making. In Canada in 1997 boards barely had one [4] non-executive director who was an industry insider. Today almost four [4] directors in the boards can be considered as industry experts. "Industry insiders represented close to half (43%) of all incoming directors" [4] on Canadian boards in 2011.

The industry preference is also evident in the appointment of international directors (Figure 7.4). Foreign CEOs in Indian companies mostly had vast experience in the same business as that of the company: More than 70% of the non-Indian directors are industry experts. Indian board members with experience not related to the company

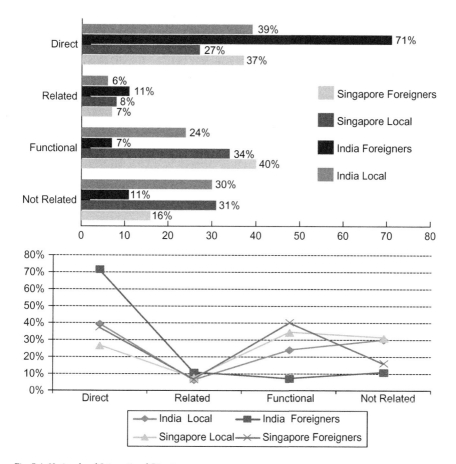

Fig. 7.4. National and International Directors.

activities are almost three times those of foreign directors. Similarly, more than one-third of foreign directors in Singapore are industry insiders, and local members with unrelated experience are double the number of non-Singaporeans.

7.6 POSITIVE EFFECT ON PERFORMANCE

The descriptive statistics (Table 7.2) show that on an average boards have directors with six or seven different types of experience and educational background. While some boards have as few as three different types of background, maximum skill diversity is 9 and 14 in Singapore and India, respectively. There is not much variation between different boards in the two countries, with the exception of educational background in India. Mean and median both indicate that Indian boards have more diversity of skill and experience than Singapore boards.

Board members with different functional, industrial, and domain expertise have a positive effect on the financial performance of companies. The mean return on assets (ROA) of India (10.45) was greater than that of Singapore (7.61), implying that the more skill diversity, the better are the returns. Companies in the top quartile (both countries together) in terms of experience diversity made, on average, 8.4% greater returns on assets than those in the bottom quartile. Boards with diverse knowledge and skill appear to have a definite and positive impact on return on assets, suggesting that greater the diversity of expertise, the better is the performance of an organization. It would thus be advisable for company boards to have members with a wide range of skills and talents.

Table 7.2. Skill Diversity in India and Singapore				
Skill Diversity	Singapore		India	
	Streams	Experiences	Streams	Experiences
Min	3	3	3	4
Max	9	9	14	12
Average	6	6	7	7
Median	5	5	7	7
Mode	5	5	7	7
Variance	3	2	5	3
Range	6	6	11	8

REFERENCES

[1] Less than 1% of FTSE 50 board directors have HR background, MAY 10, 2012, HR Review, http://www.hrreview.co.uk/hrreview-articles/hr-strategy-practice/less-than-1-of-ftse-50-board-directors-have-hr-background/35848.

[2] Hedrick and Struggles, Corporate Governance Report 2011, Challenging Board Performance.

[3] Hedrick and Struggles, Corporate Governance Report 2009, Boards in Turbulent Times.

[4] Canadian Spencer Stuart Board Index Board Trends and Practices of Leading Canadian Companies 2011.

[5] Canadian Spencer Stuart Board Index Board Trends and Practices of Leading Canadian Companies 2009 Canadian Spencer Stuart Board Index Board Trends and Practices of Leading Canadian Companies 2011.

[6] Spencer Stuart Board Index, 2011.

[7] R. Sealy, E. Doldor, V. Singh, S. Vinnicombe, Women on Boards Oct 2011, International Centre for Women Leaders, Cranfield School of Management.

[8] Canadian Spencer Stuart Board Index Board Trends and Practices of Leading Canadian Companies 2008.

[9] A. Gregoric, L. Oxelheim, T. Randøy, S. Thomsen, Corporate Governance as a Source of Competitiveness for Nordic firms, Nordic Innovation Centre, March 2009.

CHAPTER 8

Blend of Diverse Personalities

The individual directors that make up the team at the helm of corporate affairs not only need a representative spread of skills and experiences, but together must form a balanced personality of the board.

8.1 DEEP-LEVEL DIVERSITY

People with different personalities approach decisions differently. The personality of an individual is framed by his or her attitudes, attributes, social endowment, and skills. People differ not only in their interests and skills but also in the way they perceive, their reactions, values, motivations, and the way they interact and come to conclusions (Figure 8.1). Research suggests that a diversity of personality types helps "business to drive innovation, attract a wider pool of prospective candidates, improve brand image and connect to a broader range of customers" [1].

Personality diversity, or deep-level diversity, is concerned with the varying attitudes, beliefs, and value systems of people. Studies show that as teams work together, the effects of surface-level diversity tends to subside with time and deep-level diversities float up. The ultimate success of such teams is a result not only of the members' talents and resources, but also of the nature of interactions among team members. Key determinants of these interactions are the characteristics of the individual team members. Individual differences play a vital role in the success of any given team. Some of these differences are readily visible (e.g. gender, age, ethnicity), while others are not (e.g. attitudes, values, personality). Yet those characteristics that are less readily observable

The glass is half empty.
The glass is half full.
The glass is full —half with water, the
other half with air.

Fig. 8.1. Three Perceptions.

are as, if not more, important than surface-level difference. It is the soft qualities of directors that affect the functioning of boards. Even the best computer hardware won't be effective unless the right software is installed. While some characteristics may be desirable for all board members, such as confidence, self-motivation, integrity, and a sense of responsibility, having diverse personal traits will help board members take different responsibilities on the team and play various roles in the decision-making process. If all want to be stars—the opening batsman on a cricket team—the game cannot be played.

A cricket team needs 11 players, consisting of batsmen, bowlers, and fielders. While all players need stamina, team spirit, passion for the game, and a "fire in the belly" to win, the skills and personalities for each role are different. The opening batsmen in a limited over game must be aggressive and keep his wits about him so that he can score high numbers of runs. In a test match the openers are required to be patient and defensive to stay long on the crease. That is why often teams have different opening batsman for twenty-twenty matches and a test match. In one-day cricket, the batsman coming in third or fourth must be able to change his game depending on when the wickets fell. He must be a responsible player and make calculated moves. If they come early, they have to play a long careful innings, if they come a little later in the game they need to be innovative and hit a big score quickly while minimizing the risk of getting out. Middle-order batsmen are often chosen for their endurance and composure. Lower-order batsmen mostly need to make the maximum possible runs in a few

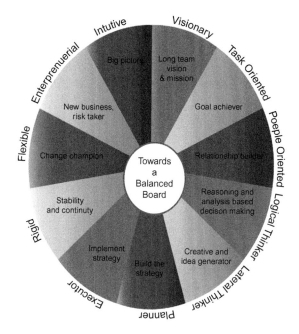

Fig. 8.2. Personality and Role.

overs. Those who enjoy the freedom to hit without any responsibility are best for this position. If you ask such players to play a steady innings and build a score for the team, they become uncomfortable. Along the same lines, the board not only needs members with different skills; like a cricket team, it must have players with different attributes who can take up different roles in the pursuit of the "big win."

8.1.1 The Players

Some of the different kinds of players that can make a "winning board" are discussed below (Figure 8.2).

Visionary vs short-term: While a visionary will hold a long-term view and see the bigger picture, creating the long-term mission of the company, those with a short-term perspective will ensure that the firm's current objectives are met. It is the vision of N. R. Narayana Murthy, founder of Infosys, that put India at the center stage of information technology in the world arena.

Problem solver vs devil's advocate: While the board definitely needs people who can solve problems that the company is facing and mitigate board conflicts, it also needs a devil's advocate who questions the company's systems, processes, and decisions, resulting in continuous improvement.

Logical thinker vs lateral thinker: The logical thinker is coherent in his thought process and his views will be based on analysis and a sequential flow of reasoning. The lateral thinker will be more creative and come up with new ideas.

Focused vs wanderer: While it is important to concentrate on a discussion in progress, an occasional wander may come up with spontaneous ideas as such individuals tend to engage more in the future than in the past.

Planner vs executor: Boards need directors who are good at creating strategy and long-term goals for the company, but they should also have members who can obtain resources, and monitor and ensure proper implementation of the strategy.

Rigid vs flexible: Boards must be flexible, adapting to new ideas and change, but they must stand their ground when it matters. The success of Starbucks Coffee shops is attributed to their ability to "challenge the old way of doing things."

Assertive vs collaborative: Boards must have assertive directors who can exercise control over management, but they must also have directors who have an understanding, appreciation, and tolerance of all people and for nature. Through their collaborative approach they should bring together all stakeholders—shareholders, directors, employees, and customers—toward one goal: the welfare of all.

Entrepreneurial vs risk averse: The board needs directors with an entrepreneurial bent, who can identify opportunities, take risks, and build new businesses. The team must also have members who can recognize and caution against too much risk.

Task oriented vs people oriented: Some people are primarily concerned with accomplishing the task at hand, while others are concerned with how well people work together. People-oriented directors are likely to consider the impact of decisions on different stakeholders and look for alternatives that are balanced in the interest of all. The success of Infosys is credited to its excellent customer service backed by highly talented people who were rewarded by the ownership of the company through stock options.

Organized vs spontaneous: Boards require directors who are structured and able to do things in a well-planned and organized manner, but times of chaos and turmoil call for directors who are creatively stimulated by a dynamic environment filled with uncertainties. The success of the discount store Walmart is attributed to the efficiency of its systems coupled with an ability to innovate.

Analytical vs intuitive: Analytical directors rely on facts and figures and have an eye for details. Intuitive directors rely on their gut feeling and tend to be big-picture thinkers; they are the idea generators. Both the big picture and the details are needed when determining processes, procedures, or best practices. It was Steve Jobs' intuition for emerging technologies that created products like the iPad, but without the pragmatism of Tim Cook, Apple would not have achieved such success.

8.1.2 A Performing Board

A combination of different traits is required for a board to be effective. As each individual will have a different mix of characteristics when appointing members, a balance must be sought. "Once asked what his best business decision was, [Bill] Gates replied without hesitation that it came down to picking people. 'Deciding to go into business with Paul Allen is probably at the top of the list, and subsequently hiring a friend, Steve Ballmer [Gates' successor as CEO at Microsoft]. It's important to have someone who you totally trust, who is totally committed, who shares your vision, yet who has a little bit different set of skills and who also acts as something of a check on you'" [2].

If all directors are idea generators, who will implement those ideas? If the cricket team already has good spinners, appointing more may be of no use; instead, a medium or fast bowler would strengthen the team. "Marks & Spencer's 1999 share-price collapse is believed to have been partly caused by the decision of then-CEO Sir Richard Greenbury to surround himself exclusively with 'M&S clones' allowing ideas to saturate in a stagnant 'groupthink'" [1].

An effective board is one that can successfully perform its functions of governance, strategic direction, and supervision. This requires a

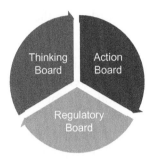

Fig. 8.3. A Holistic Board.

balanced board that can think, act, and regulate. What good is a board that comes out with a brilliant plan that can take the company to the top but fails to implement it properly? Without a good plan, no matter what the board does there will be no long-term growth and sustainability. Hence the thinking board needs visionaries, intellectuals, and creative people. The action board requires organizers, executors, and task-focused members. The regulatory board must have an eye for detail, and it must be firm and systematic. Thus, a holistic board that can carry out its role and responsibilities successfully must have members with diverse personalities (Figure 8.3).

8.2 LEVERAGING PERSONALITY DIVERSITY

Board directors must appreciate the need for diverse personalities and respect each other. For a board to strive for excellence, the strengths and limitations of each member are to be understood and leveraged in the best possible way. A risk taker should not be asked to oversee internal control mechanisms, nor should a task master be put in charge of building stakeholder relationships, just as a batsman who only likes to take big hits should not be made the opening batsman.

The board chair has a major role here. He must have the necessary skills to manage diverse personalities. Just as the captain of a cricket team should choose a batting order most conducive for the individual players, enabling the team to perform its best, chairpersons, instead of expecting everyone to conform to a common norm, should be able to utilize the strengths of different personalities to the advantage of the board. Each player is critical to the team. Although each member is a "star" in his or her own right, it is the leadership of the board chair that motivates them to work as a team toward a common goal.

Above all, the interest of the company must be foremost in the minds of the directors. Rahul Dravid, the well-known and respected Indian cricketer, "always put team above himself. He did everything his team wanted or required him to do. Though he was a middle-order batsman, he opened the batting in Test matches when the team fell short of competent openers. He donned the wicket-keeping gloves in ODIs so that his team could afford to go with an extra batsman or a bowler. He batted at different positions as per the team's requirement" [3]. Directors too must wear the cap of the role that is required by the situation.

REFERENCES

[1] Businesses need to recruit more smartly to improve diversity, Ora Ruth Rother 12 October 2011   <http://www.personneltoday.com/articles/2011/10/12/58022/businesses-need-to-recruit-more-smartly-to-improve-diversity.html>.

[2] The 12 greatest entrepreneurs of our time, <http://money.cnn.com/galleries/2012/news/companies/1203/gallery.greatest-entrepreneurs.fortune/index.html>.

[3] Can Rahul Dravid coach the Indian cricket team? <http://cricketnext.in.com/live/news/can-rahul-dravid-coach-the-indian-cricket-team/66693-13.html>.

Building an Effective Board

Successful boards are those that choose the right combination of hetero-geneous directors and, by correctly managing the complexities of diver-sity, leverage those differences to their advantage.

9.1 VALUE-ADDING BOARDS

A board may prove to be one of the following: a board that creates negative value (deteriorates the company from its earlier position); a board that creates no value (ensures compliance and maintains the sta-tus quo); or a board that creates value (through vision and strategic guidance). Every board desires and strives to be a "value creator." They all want to live up to the expectations placed on them. They want to create great companies, companies that are not just "tracked by history" but that "create history." A far-sighted board with a strong character and the ability to do things differently can do that. This calls for a board with a vibrant personality, a 360-degree view capable of taking complex decisions in trying situations and making sure that those decisions are implemented, yet quickly changing these very deci-sions if circumstances change. As discussed earlier, such a board needs to be made of members who are heterogeneous in terms of personality, gender, age, race, nationality, education, and experience. Although diversity is logical and intuitively sound for enhancing board perfor-mance, a view that has become widely accepted, empirical findings have not been that convincing.

9.2 DIVERSITY VIEWS

A study [1] based on interviews with directors found that while everyone agreed that diversity was good for boards, as it brought different perspectives, few could pinpoint specific benefits gained from diversity. Benefits from having women and minorities were particularly not very obvious, but many instances were stated where the particular skills and experience of a director proved very useful. In one instance, a woman director was not sure whether her ability to bring people to a common solution was her "motherly skill" or her "lawyer skill." There were a few examples given where women directors were better able to understand needs of women customers, and board discussion moved from the strictly financial to the board's impact on employees and long-term perspectives.

In a small survey* of directors (all male) done by the authors, a few felt that women make some difference, as they had a different perspective or "inlay at issue." One respondent commented that gender diversity improves the "democratic line of thinking." While some directors felt that women directors did not add value, others emphasized the need for women having the "right skill." One gave names of well-known women CEOs and said that women of caliber could make a significant difference to boards.

When asked about the impact a foreign director would have on decision making, most felt it would not be significant. Concerns put forth were that foreigners would not understand "Indian conditions," or not "adjust with Indian boards," and boards would be required to "design new processes." One respondent was of the view that having a foreign director is not required, as "there is enough expertise in the country." Some did state that directors from other countries would bring "new idea," "new approach," and a "rich experience"; others suggested that they would be particularly useful for globalizing business operations. There was also a comment that foreign directors would make the board more independent.

On responding to the question of the benefits of having more young directors on a board, most directors responded positively. In addition to new ideas, they referred to the young directors' energy levels,

*This is based on part of an initial survey conducted by Dr. Shital Jhunjhunwala during November/December 2012 in India to study board functioning.

dynamism, risk-taking approach, and the fact that they were "conversant to IT and capacity to adapt new technology." There was some apprehension about lack of experience.

Most directors expressed that having a mix of old and new directors would be beneficial for the board by adding "new blood to the board" and providing continuity for the board, but they cautioned against "frequent changes."

There was a general consensus that boards with members from different educational and experiential backgrounds improved board performance through a diverse knowledge base, "because all the aspects will be taken care of." One director stressed the need for boards not to be lopsided with engineers and finance experts; another went so far as to say that diversity of skill is compulsory for ensuring "sustainability" of the company. This correlates with our findings (refer to Chapter 7) that boards with diversity of skill and experience perform better.

9.3 BUILDING THE RIGHT BOARD

As Rosen and Dysart [2] put it, board members meet four times a year, perhaps eight times in some of the more active boards. They come as individuals, all of them achievers in their own right. They do not get the time to spend together to create a common culture and feeling of oneness. They have to plan and take decisions in a short span of time, but they do not have much in the way of resources allotted to them. They are responsible to shareholders but it is the CEO and his team who run the show. Yet they must be effective. Selection of the right members is thus critical.

We have seen in the previous chapters the different aspects of board diversity and how they impact board performance. The way the board performs is influenced by the type of directors it has. The board should be formed of individuals who are highly talented, dynamic, and geared up to face today's challenging and ever-changing business environment. For the complex role of boards, a balanced team of heterogeneous directors is required. Diversity "just for the heck of it" will not be beneficial. A SWOT analysis of the board will determine its competency to meet current business challenges and identify areas which need to be strengthened. At the same time some board members may have outlived their utilities, and it may be advisable to replace them.

Table 9.1. Choosing Board Members	
Age	• Young • Old
Gender	• Male • Female
Tenure	• Existing member • New member
Nation	• Which country? • India, USA, Middle East, etc.
Education	• What level of education is required? • Which stream—finance, marketing, law, arts, etc.?
Experience	• Functional—accounts, human resouces, operations, etc. • Industry—steel, software, pharma, real estate, etc. • Specialized—branding, IPR, designing, etc. • Company profile—small or big, new or mature, etc.
Personality	• What blend of characteristics is required? • Organized logical thinker with an analytical bent, or a spontaneous lateral thinker with a collobrative approach?

Historically, not much thought has been given to the talent gap on boards and how to overcome them. The selection of board members must be based on a set of appropriate criteria, a performance review of each director, and a talent gap analysis (Table 9.1). What skills and traits are needed but lacking in the current board? Are all the members over 60 years of age? Is a younger and more energetic person needed? What functional experience is required? Are we planning new acquisitions, and should the board have a lawyer with expertise in mergers and acquisitions? Is the company planning to expand to the Middle East? Will it be useful to have someone who understands that market? Such questions need to be answered before considering appointing members to board.

The results of an analysis might show that the board needs a member who has the traits, skills, and competencies shown in Figure 9.1. Then efforts may be made to find a member who fits the bill. The selection process should be structured and involve all stakeholders. While it may not be possible to find an exact fit, the best possible candidate must be selected.

Ultimately, what is important is the unique contribution each potential broad member will bring to the table. The focus must be on what is to be achieved by board diversity. The aim must be to have a broad talent base. There is no ideal mix of directors: It depends on the

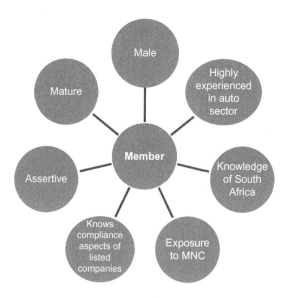

Fig. 9.1. Required Candidate Example.

needs of the company and its business. It is important to understand the talents and skills that will be needed in the future and plan accordingly. *Just like employee management, board talent must be strategically managed to build a competent board with diverse perspectives and skills. Not just CEO succession planning but a dynamic board succession planning process must be put in place, whereby through an aggressive recruitment process top-quality members are selected based on the current and future needs.*

9.4 MAKING DIVERSITY WORK

Why does diversity not seem to work? Diverse boards no doubt will benefit from multiple perspectives and skills, but friction and communication bottlenecks may develop. Instead of new ideas and views, diversity may lead to stifled voices and dominance by few. To reap its fruits, boards must successfully manage diversity. Instead of shunning diversity, boards need to minimize the conflict that diversity often introduces and learn to respect and work with colleagues who are selected because they are *different* [3] (see Box 1: Diverse Boards at Work).

Conflicts can be avoided by clearly defining the process, roles, and expectations and building mutual trust among members. Leadership

Box 1 Diverse Boards at Work

Alliances on the Los Angeles Board of Education are fluid, delicate and often unpredictable.

For example, while Leticia Quezada has counted Jackie Goldberg on her side when it comes to bilingual education and year-round schools, it is a different matter when the issue is whether to change superintendents or how to lop $220 million from the Los Angeles Unified School District's annual budget.

These days, the most consistent allies are Rita Walters and Quezada, who often stand together on matters they believe reflect inequities in the treatment of black and Latino students.

That was not always the case. Quezada said Walters did not trust her when she first joined the board, and the two engaged in some public feuding. Eventually, they worked out their differences during several private meetings, including one at the home of Los Angeles City Councilman Richard Alatorre.

"We broke down the barriers between them," Alatorre said of the afternoon session. "We had two strong-willed women very committed to issues. They had the same concerns, but they weren't communicating."

Walters, 60, a fiery veteran of school desegregation battles, has long believed that the district's black youngsters get a raw deal. She is openly suspicious of the other board members' motives. She refused to vote for fellow liberal Goldberg for president, and sometimes needles Warren Furutani, whose dramatically diverse board district stretches from the poor black and Latino neighborhoods south of Los Angeles to the suburb of San Pedro: "Warren, you act like you don't represent Watts."

Quezada, 37, came to California as a child, a Mexican immigrant struggling to learn English in schools that had little help to offer her. She graduated with honors from UC Santa Cruz, and earned a master's degree in education and a teaching credential.

High on her priorities list are bilingual education and more Latino parent involvement in the schools. A diplomat who talks about "process," she refrains from personal criticism of other board members and tries to get along with all her colleagues.

Goldberg, 46, an articulate, longtime liberal activist, is philosophically aligned with Quezada and Walters, but she often positions herself to be more open to compromise, especially on the kind of trade-off issues she calls "tweeners." She sided with the majority (and against Walters and Quezada) in a vote to relax the district's tough academic requirements for participation in sports and other after-school activities because she felt the activities' incentives for youngsters to stay in school outweighed the need for maintaining strict achievement rules.

Furutani, 43, shot into the spotlight in 1987 when he reversed his vote on a plan to relieve overcrowding by putting all the district's schools into year-round operation. His reversal forced the board to delay its plan. Fellow board members criticized his "flip-flop," some contending that he had not understood what he had voted on.

Furutani said his constituents did not know about the vote and had not been given the opportunity to "register their feelings." This year, he voted for the proposal--after holding six neighborhood meetings.

Since the 1987 flap, he has kept a relatively low profile, viewing himself as a "mediator" and putting few controversial measures on the table. He is sometimes a swing vote, and sides more often with the suburban members.

Julie Korenstein, 47, elected with strong union support, has found common ground most often with another union ally and the board's newest member, Mark Slavkin, elected in 1989 to represent the Westside. They sit next to each other at board meetings, and she often seems to consult him before she speaks out or moves to amend others' motions.

A former special education teacher, Korenstein has carried the ball on successful drives to toughen the district's punishment of students who bring weapons to school and to soften its academic standards for students who participate in extracurricular activities.

An avowed fiscal conservative, she has set herself up as a watchdog of district spending, and often questions even small amounts for building projects or field trips. She has been dismissed by some as a lightweight, in part because her questions are often simplistic and appear to reflect a lack of understanding of district procedures. She is lauded by others for not being afraid to question "sacred cows" or challenge conventional notions, such as her suggestion earlier this year that the district's busing-for-integration program be disbanded because its students were not showing achievement gains.

Many board watchers expect Slavkin, at 29 its youngest member, to go the furthest in carving out a political career. A former aide to county Supervisor Ed Edelman, his political sophistication shows in his demeanor and the broad approach he has taken in his short time on the board.

has an important role here. It is the chairperson who sets the tone and coordinates the working of the board. Although the chairperson is not the "boss," he is the facilitator of the board. The chairperson must be able to involve everyone in discussions and quickly resolve conflicts. He or she should ensure smooth interactions among the individual members and guide them toward a common goal—the interests of the company and its stakeholders. It is up to the board chair to get the best out of members by appropriately capitalizing on their different knowledge and skills for maximum board performance. Success or failure of the board is determined by the chairperson effectively managing board dynamism.

Often the new member is stereotyped (e.g. "that's a typical woman response") and finds it difficult to be accepted as a positive contributor. Such newcomers then become reluctant to share their views. Efforts must be made to align new members with the board philosophy and processes right at the beginning. On one hand, boards need to be open-minded and willing to accept "others"; on the other hand, newcomers should work at winning over skeptical members. Just as new employees have an orientation process, there must be a formal process of induction for new board members.

Communication is another critical factor that influences the boards' effectiveness. Body language, tone of voice, and facial expression are as important as words. While constructive arguments are an integral part of any decision-making process, such disagreements should not become personal battles. Board discussions should take place in a constructive environment, in which members talk to each other, not against each other, or to the chairman.

Cohesion among members is vital. Cohesion, however, does not mean uniformity of background or nature. The feeling of unity in diversity is essential. No subgroups should be formed. A spirit of oneness among directors and a willingness to work together in the interest of the company's stakeholders will ensure that the board is able to give the best results. It is about board chemistry where members co-create strategy and decision making. A well-functioning board is one in which members trust each other, share a common value for the company, encourage divergent opinions, and come to decisions without clashes.

To enhance board performance and create value that diverse boards can generate, members must:

Recognize the diversities.
Appreciate and respect the diversities.
Learn to work as a team, irrespective of diversity.
Leverage the diversity.

REFERENCES

[1] L.L. Broome, J.M. Conley, K.D. Krawiec, Dangerous Categories: Narratives of Corporate Board Diversity https://ddi.law.unc.edu/documents/boarddiversity/broomeconleykrawiec8.2.10. pdf.

[2] R. Rosen, T.L. Dysart, The board as a team: It takes the right framework, Heidrick & Struggles Governance Letter, http://www.heidrick.com/PublicationsReports/PublicationsReports/HS_Gov_Letter_30th_Anniv.pdf.

[3] J.-F. Manzoni, P. Strebel, J.-L. Barsoux, Why Diversity Can Backfire On Company Boards June 14, 2012, The Wall Street Journal, http://online.wsj.com/article/SB1000142405274870355800457458185108902682.html.

Printed and bound by CPI Group (UK) Ltd, Croydon, CR0 4YY

08/05/2025

01864771-0002